EMERGING MACROFISCAL AND GOVERNANCE CHALLENGES AND OPPORTUNITIES IN DEVELOPING ASIA AND THE PACIFIC

Gambhir Bhatta, Dennis Lorne Nacario, and Jose Luis Syquia

MARCH 2026

ASIAN DEVELOPMENT BANK

6 ADB Avenue, Mandaluyong City, 1550 Metro Manila, Philippines
Tel +63 2 8632 4444; Fax +63 2 8636 2444
www.adb.org

ISBN 978-92-9277-736-4 (print); 978-92-9277-737-1 (PDF); 978-92-9277-738-8 (ebook)
Publication Stock No. TCS260103-2
DOI: http://dx.doi.org/10.22617/TCS260103-2

Notes:
In this publication, "$" refers to United States dollars, "€" refers to euros, "NRs" refers to Nepalese rupees, and "GEL" refers to lari.
ADB recognizes "Vietnam" as Viet Nam.

All photos by ADB.

Cover design by Editha Creus.

Contents

Tables, Figures, and Boxes

Tables

Figures

Boxes

Foreword

Over the past 50 years, Asia and the Pacific has achieved substantial economic and social progress. More than 1.5 billion people have moved out of poverty, and digitalization has expanded access to essential services. Despite these gains, the region faces complex challenges, including rising climate and disaster risks, geopolitical uncertainty, persistent gaps in access to basic services, and the lingering effects of recent shocks. Weak macrofiscal management, poor policy choices, and limited political commitment continue to undermine governance in some countries.

The Asian Development Bank's (ADB) Strategy 2030 and its midterm review reaffirm that strong macrofiscal frameworks and effective governance are essential to achieving a prosperous, inclusive, resilient, and sustainable Asia and the Pacific. Strong public financial management, effective domestic resource mobilization, prudent debt management, and capable institutions are critical to progress in key areas, including climate action, private sector development, regional cooperation and public goods, digital transformation, and resilience and empowerment.

This report—*Emerging Macrofiscal and Governance Challenges and Opportunities in Developing Asia and the Pacific*—examines three interconnected pillars that shape macrofiscal and governance performance in the region: (a) domestic resource mobilization and debt management, (b) public financial and expenditure management, and (c) oversight and accountability mechanisms. The analysis draws on ADB country diagnostics, analytical work, operational experience, and discussions at the inaugural Workshop on Emerging Governance and Macrofiscal Issues and Opportunities, held at ADB headquarters in Manila on 18–19 September 2025. The workshop discussions underscored the need for integrated and context-specific approaches to governance reform across ADB's developing member countries.

Consistent with the report's findings, stronger collaboration, greater inclusiveness, sustained political commitment, and a holistic approach to reforms are essential. I trust this study will contribute to policy dialogue and support efforts to strengthen institutions, improve governance systems, and enhance macrofiscal resilience across the region.

Tariq Niazi
Senior Director
Public Sector Management and Governance Sector Office
Sectors Department 3
Asian Development Bank

About the Authors

Gambhir Bhatta is the former Chief of the Governance Thematic Group at the Asian Development Bank (ADB). He took early retirement from the bank in 2021, after which he has been providing consulting services to various clients across the world, including the UN in New York, and G2G Inc. in Wellington. He has continued to consult regularly with ADB in various areas, including evaluation capacity development, governance and public sector management, knowledge management, and MEL (monitoring, evaluation, and learning).

From 2016 to 2025, he was an adjunct faculty member at the Lee Kuan Yew School of Public Policy (Singapore). Prior to joining ADB in 2005, Gambhir was a Senior Advisor at the State Services Commission in New Zealand.

Gambhir is the author of several books, including *'Those that fix the lights'... The Practice of Public Sector Management in Developing Asia* (ADB, ADB Institute, and Routledge, 2020); and *International Dictionary of Public Management and Governance* (M. E. Sharpe, Inc., New York, 2006). He has a doctorate degree in Public and International Affairs, with specialization in Applied Policy Analysis, from the University of Pittsburgh.

Jose Luis Syquia is a Principal Public Sector Specialist in ADB's Sectors Department 3 – Public Sector Management and Governance Sector Office (SD3-PSMG). He leads SD3-PSMG's Strategy, Emerging Areas and Knowledge team, and handles policy-based operations that introduce reforms in the areas of public financial management and fiscal sustainability, enabling environments for private sector development, climate and disaster resilience, state-owned enterprise reforms, and asset management. He also designed and rolled out ADB's Governance and Macrofiscal Pillars assessment methodology, which informs ADB's country partnership strategies and programmatic pipelines for developing member countries.

Prior to this, Joel was the Unit Head for Due Diligence at ADB's Office of Anticorruption and Integrity, and a Senior Procurement Specialist at ADB's Procurement, Portfolio and Financial Management Department. He also served as Legal Officer and Procurement Lead at the Global Fund to Fight AIDS, Tuberculosis and Malaria in Geneva, Switzerland.

Joel holds a master's degree in law and was an ACAMS Certified Anti-Money Laundering Specialist. He has 27 years of professional experience in governance, public sector management, law, integrity, and procurement.

Dennis Lorne Nacario is a governance, public procurement, and public financial management expert with extensive experience in conducting ADB's country diagnostics on governance and public financial management across Asia and the Pacific. He also provided consultancy services on public procurement and capacity building for development partners, such as UNDP, USAID, and GIZ, contributing to green public procurement, procurement monitoring systems, and various institutional reforms.

Dennis previously served as Deputy Executive Director of the Government Procurement Policy Board–Technical Support Office in the Philippines and as a Procurement Specialist with the Millennium Challenge Account–Philippines. He holds a Juris Doctor degree and multiple public procurement specialist certifications.

Acknowledgments

The authors thank Taylor & Francis Group for granting permission to reproduce selected copyright material from the 2020 book *Those That Fix the Lights: The Practice of Public Sector Management in Developing Asia* (Gambhir Bhatta; Asian Development Bank [ADB], Routledge, and Asian Development Bank Institute) by Gambhir Bhatta, published by Asian Development Bank (ADB), ADB Institute, and Routledge."

At ADB, the authors thank Tariq Niazi, Senior Director, Public Sector Management and Governance (PSMG) Sector Office, for leading PSMG's work program, which underpins this study. The support and guidance from Navendu Karan, Director, PSMG, for the inaugural Workshop on Emerging Governance and Macrofiscal Issues and Opportunities, held at ADB headquarters in Manila on 18–19 September 2025 is immensely appreciated. During the workshop, officials from selected ADB developing member countries discussed many of the issues examined in this report.

The authors also acknowledge Cigdem Akin, Director, PSMG, for helping integrate the issues discussed at the workshop into a coherent narrative within PSMG's work program and for identifying practical responses to them.

ADB experts and participating government officials provided valuable insights on fiscal risks, domestic resource mobilization, private sector development, and other PSMG areas. The following ADB experts deserve thanks for their contributions: Laisiasa Tora, Sandeep Bhattacharya, Rachana Shrestha, Saad Abdullah Paracha, Nyda Mukhtar, Dayna Connolly, and Chieko Yokota.

The authors also thank the anonymous reviewers for their constructive comments on the draft manuscript.

Abbreviations

ADB	Asian Development Bank
BEPS	base erosion and profit shifting
CCET	Climate Change Expenditure Tagging
CDR	climate and disaster resilience
CIAA	Commission for the Investigation of Abuse of Authority
CIPS	Chartered Institute of Procurement & Supply
COA	Commission on Audit
COVID-19	coronavirus disease 2019
CPA	country performance assessment
CPS	country partnership strategy
CSO	civil society organization
DMC	developing member country
DRM	domestic resource mobilization
e-GP	electronic government procurement
FMIS	financial management information system
GDP	gross domestic product
GESI	gender equality and social inclusion
GMaP	governance and macrofiscal pillar
GRB	gender-responsive budgeting
GRPFM	gender-responsive public financial management
iBAS++	Integrated Budget and Accounting System
IA	information asymmetry
IFRS	International Financial Reporting Standards
II	imperfect information
IMF	International Monetary Fund
IPSAS	International Public Sector Accounting Standards
ICT	information and communication technology
M&E	monitoring and evaluation
MDB	multilateral development bank
MIRA	Maldives Inland Revenue Authority
MOF	Ministry of Finance
MTBF	medium-term budgetary framework
MTEF	medium-term expenditure framework
MTFF	medium-term fiscal framework
NGO	nongovernment organization
NIS	national integrity strategy
OAG	Office of the Auditor General
ODA	overseas development assistance

OECD	Organisation for Economic Co-operation and Development
PAC	Public Accounts Committee
PDR	People's Democratic Republic
PEFA	Public Expenditure and Financial Accountability
PFM	public financial management
PIM	public investment management
PIMA	Public Investment Management Assessment
PPMO	Public Procurement Monitoring Office
PPP	public–private partnership
PSD	private sector development
PSM	public sector management
PSMG	public sector management and governance
RMI	Republic of the Marshall Islands
SAI	state audit institution
SDG	Sustainable Development Goals
SME	small and medium-sized enterprise
SNG	subnational government
SOE	state-owned enterprise
SusPP	sustainable public procurement
TSA	treasury single account
UNCTAD	United Nations Conference on Trade and Development
VAT	value-added tax

Executive Summary

Despite phenomenal economic and social progress in Asia and the Pacific in the last half century, further improvements in the macrofiscal and governance domains could be made. This study considers the various issues and challenges facing 34 developing member countries (DMCs) of the Asian Development Bank (ADB) in strengthening public sector management and governance (PSMG). The primary question posed is: *What macrofiscal and governance challenges do DMCs currently face, and how can these be addressed in a manner that is consistent with individual country contexts?*

Primary Concepts Discussed

Using a systems perspective on macrofiscal and governance considerations, the study homes in on a whole-of-government approach to enhance policy coherence and account for trade-offs, among others. On the issue of strengthened governance, the study also considers two associated concepts: country systems, and macrofiscal and governance pillars. The former accounts for national arrangements and procedures for public financial management (PFM), that is, budgeting, treasury, accounting, auditing, reporting, and procurement to achieve a country's development goals, while the latter refers to domestic resource mobilization (DRM) and debt management, public financial and expenditure management, and oversight and accountability as foundations for strong macrofiscal frameworks and good governance.

Results Chain in Governance

The stylized results chain implicit in ADB's work on PSMG is revealing in that its strategic priorities (themselves anchored on several factors of instrumentation) lead to systemic outcomes, which can be considered as pathways that enable governments to achieve their respective long-term development visions. Three systemic outcome areas are emphasized in the study: DRM and debt management; public financial and expenditure management; and oversight and accountability mechanisms. The overarching domains within which policy actions in the public space play out include subnational governance, the role of the private sector, capacity development, and infrastructure governance, among others.

Strategic priorities in each of these outcomes are numerous and include, for example, e-procurement, accountability of processes, resources and results, robust medium-term fiscal and expenditure frameworks, and management of fiscal risks. Examples of instrumentation include digitalization, access to information, gender-responsive budgeting, and the use of analytical tools such as public expenditure and financial accountability assessments.

Meaningful Reform Programs Across the Three Pillars

The study's findings clearly show that it is only by managing reforms across multiple fronts that governments can effectively and efficiently deliver public services, successfully respond to economic crises and other shocks, and achieve and sustain macrofiscal stability. A meaningful reform program needs to prioritize and sequence legal, regulatory, and institutional strengthening measures across these pillars:

(a) *Domestic resource mobilization and debt management:* increased mobilization of domestic resources will not only reduce the need to issue domestic debt but will also address possible overreliance on external debt, which may undermine the use of fiscal and monetary policy.

(b) *Public financial and expenditure management:* effective public financial and public expenditure management are at the core of a government's ability to utilize public resources to achieve impactful development outcomes by ensuring that public sector planning, budgeting, and execution benefit from aggregate fiscal discipline, and allocative as well as operational efficiency.

(c) *Oversight and accountability mechanisms:* as good governance is characterized by accountable public institutions, it is imperative to strengthen the government's accountability mechanisms. The roles of the legislature and state audit institutions need to be complemented by effective anticorruption institutions and robust civil society engagement as critical elements of meaningful governance reforms.

Emerging Issues, Challenges, and Opportunities

The study flags emerging PSMG policy issues and challenges in various areas in ADB's DMCs.

Strengthening subnational governance. From localizing the global development agenda to improving local governance, subnational PFM institutions and practices, service delivery, and accountability, both from a political and political economy perspective, the need to strengthen subnational governance has never been of greater exigency. Among the key issues identified in the study are: (a) a systemic disconnect and strategic misalignment across plans, projects, and budgets at the local level; (b) a general lack of transparency in the policy space, which is a foundational enabler of strong local governance; and (c) a tendency to adopt a one-size-fits-all approach to PFM reforms at the subnational level.

Enhancing domestic resource mobilization. There are realistic limits to the levels of foreign direct investment and official development assistance flowing to DMCs. Coupled with exogenous trends, such as loss of trade preferences and concessional financing, this has logically necessitated greater reliance on domestic revenue generation, strategic expenditure planning, and fiscal consolidation. Robust tax policy and effective tax administration measures definitely help but the study flags other measures to mobilize a higher level of domestic resources, including: (a) minimizing revenue losses due to tax avoidance, and increased use of digital technology; (b) reforming state-owned enterprises; (c) initiating substantive public procurement reforms; (d) stemming illicit financial outflows from DMCs; and (e) making better use by national and subnational governments of publicly owned commercial assets. There are other measures that governments can consider, such as strengthening the public investment management regime.

Improving public financial and public expenditure systems. The study identifies numerous issues that merit the attention of governments: (a) weak legislative frameworks, for example, in intergovernmental fiscal arrangements and relationships, and PFM systems across multiple levels of government; (b) weak provisions in the establishment of expenditure and revenue management systems; (c) lapses in public procurement provisions, particularly in market practices, and integrity systems; (d) weak budget credibility stemming from, among others, inadequately prepared medium-term expenditure and fiscal frameworks; and (e) inadequate legislative oversight, which is a cornerstone of fiscal discipline and public accountability.

Managing fiscal risks. The issue of fiscal risks is severe for most DMCs. The risks emanate from a variety of factors, such as a high degree of contingent liabilities without adequate budget coverage. The study points to the need for considering several key issues, such as (a) vulnerable PFM processes; (b) weak accounting systems and poor internal controls inherent in public agencies; and (c) poor enforcement of fiscal rules leading to fiscal indiscipline.

Facilitating private sector development. Ambitious DMC development goals can only be achieved together with the active participation of, and engagement with, the private sector. The study identifies numerous issues impacting private sector development (PSD). To begin with, there is a need for productive consultations between the private sector and governments since these are the foundation upon which trust is built, policy effectiveness is ensured, and a stable and predictable environment for private investment is created. Investment-friendly policies and strong institutions that strengthen the rule of law are also needed, coupled with efforts to enhance digitalization and lessen unnecessary bureaucracy. The central point is that PSD is closely associated with the strength of the public sector.

Maximizing digitalization for effective service delivery. Digitalization – and information and communication technology, in general – is important for purposes of governance enhancement. It helps improve transparency, and governments need to robustly champion its role in governance reforms. However, several constraints to effective digitalization exist, such as: (a) a lack of clear and up-to-date policies that specifically address the unique requirements of digitalization in all aspects of the economy; (b) inadequate regulations for data privacy and security; (c) independent "siloed" systems that are developed by government agencies over time (e.g., for debt management, budget, and taxes) where legacy systems often do not communicate with one another, thus preventing a unified view of public finances and hindering a whole-of-government approach; (d) sub-optimal collaboration among public sector agencies; and (e) the inability of governments to go beyond the "technology fallacy," that is, the common misconception that technology is a complete solution in itself.

Focusing on climate and disaster resilience. DMCs face increasing environmental pressures from climate change. Specific roles and mandates need to be established to build an effective country platform that responds to ambitious climate targets, particularly for subnational governments and the private sector. DMCs also need to prioritize disaster risk management, and efforts need to be centered on, among others: (a) robust policy, institutional, and regulatory measures; and (b) disaster risk financing, including measures that leverage private sector investments. Investments in these areas provide far-reaching effects if they are carefully integrated into the development process.

Institutionalizing gender equality and social inclusion (GESI). GESI issues at the country level can be considered from various angles, including: (a) the principle of equality and non-discrimination; (b) fundamental rights of individuals; (c) the policy of "leave no one behind"; (d) the protection of women from different forms of violence, exploitation, or discrimination; and (e) the rights of specific disadvantaged groups to participate in state functions and to have equal access to public services. To institutionalize GESI in a country's governance system, particular emphasis needs to be placed on developing gender accountable systems in all tiers of governments. There is also a general understanding that the root causes of exclusion are structurally embedded in society and take longer to address, thus making intersectionality a key aspect of GESI reform programs.

Reinforcing oversight, accountability, and integrity. One of the key components of good governance has always been accountability, that is, accountability for work carried out, resources expended, processes followed, and stated results achieved in advance, facilitated by strong oversight provisions and mechanisms. This study puts forth a particularly reformulated narrative of looking at issues of oversight and accountability by arguing for a more whole-of-government, and therefore more elevated, approach to considering issues of good governance implied in the concept of oversight and accountability. It argues for an integrity system that is considered a fundamental element of good governance, where civil society plays a pivotal role. Elevating the conversation on oversight and accountability to one of national integrity allows governments to consider a broader set of principles, action frames, and a whole-of-government approach that is deemed superior to a narrower approach that is just focused on combating corruption. The bottom line is that the fight against malgovernance cannot be won by prosecution alone or by more rules, but rather by taking an inclusive approach based on values, ethics, and integrity in the public sector.

Pathways for Reforms in PSM and Governance

The study identifies three vectors of opportunities (i.e., reform spaces, or pathways) that could be considered to strengthen PSMG in countries. The first vector consists of a set of opportunities inherent in strengthened country systems, greater macrofiscal stability, and greater private sector development. The second, which inherently draws from the first set, is focused on opportunities contained in governments' strategic priorities (e.g., accountability, inclusiveness, fiscal discipline, fiscal transparency, and credible commitment to private sector development). Finally, the third vector is a set of opportunities focused on the instruments that governments can use to meet higher-level objectives, such as instituting a national integrity system. Analysis of these various vectors yields four specific frames of action that governments may consider. *Frame 1,* at the most direct level, provides for strategic support and capacity building for entities that are directly associated with all relevant operations. *Frame 2* focuses on greater engagement with all entities that have a bearing on government operations, as a way of ensuring that everyone understands what is transpiring in the country and how lapses can be addressed. *Frame 3* targets areas where advocacy can be enhanced across countries. Finally, *Frame 4* revolves around a better understanding of how PSMG is practiced on the ground.

Conclusion

Regardless of which frame of action is taken, experiences in strategizing and implementing reforms across DMCs have generated a number of insights:

(a) Working collaboratively and strategically with all development actors (including subnational governments) yields better results, particularly in areas where reforms tend to be difficult.
(b) Greater focus on inclusiveness, broadly defined, will yield development outcomes that are more desirable. Here, consideration of intersectionality in reform efforts is critical.
(c) An aggressive knowledge enhancement agenda with robust information systems as anchors, as well as greater impetus on facilitating data and information access, lies at the heart of all governance reform efforts. Accountability of development results rests on the effectiveness of such an agenda.
(d) The insight has to do with a strong and enduring "political commitment" to PSMG reforms. Indeed, such commitment is a necessary and sufficient condition for successful governance reforms in DMCs.

Part A. Introduction

Background

Countries in the Asia and Pacific region have made phenomenal economic and social progress in the last half century. Millions of people have been able to exit poverty, and national economies have been strengthened on many fronts. However, as Strategy 2030 of the Asian Development Bank (ADB) poignantly pointed out: "there are unfinished development agendas.... Issues such as poverty and vulnerability, rising inequality, climate change, growing environmental pressures, and large infrastructure deficits remain to be addressed."[1] Also, macrofiscal and good governance policies and arrangements across the region need to be strengthened. The midterm review of Strategy 2030 (carried out in 2024) reinforces the messages related to the underlying importance of governance, good public financial management systems, and strong institutions.[2]

Existing literature on macrofiscal arrangements highlights the centrality of transparent and well-governed institutions. ADB, in talking up the idea of the Asian Century, maintained back in 2011 that "the greatest challenge Asia faces in its endeavors to realize the Asian Century is transforming governance and institutions."[3] There is universal agreement that good governance continues to be an essential condition for governments to achieve their development goals. Indeed, Rozenberg and Fay (2019) assert governance even "trumps innovation."[4]

Scope of Coverage

This study considers the various issues and challenges in strengthening public sector management and governance (PSMG) in 34 developing member countries (DMCs) of ADB (**Appendix 1**). The primary question is: What macrofiscal and governance challenges do DMCs currently face, and how can these be addressed in a manner that is consistent with individual country contexts? In answering this question, the study also looks at reform opportunities in various PSMG domains that governments may prioritize.

For purposes of this study, the PSMG domains consist of several elements that are included in ADB's country performance assessment (CPA) exercise. In the main, these can be framed as being in four clusters: (a) *Cluster A* on economic management, (b) *Cluster B* on structural policies, (c) *Cluster C* on policies for social inclusion and equity, and (d) *Cluster D* on governance.[5]

1 Asian Development Bank (ADB). 2018a. *Strategy 2030: Achieving a Prosperous, Inclusive, Resilient, and Sustainable Asia and the Pacific*.
2 ADB. 2024a. *Strategy 2030 Midterm Review: An Evolution Approach for the Asian Development Bank*.
3 ADB. 2011. *Asia 2050: Realizing the Asian Century*. p. 93.
4 J. Rozenberg and M. Fay. 2019. *Beyond the Gap: How Countries Can Afford the Infrastructure They Need While Protecting the Planet*. Washington, DC: World Bank. p. 20.
5 Used synonymously with "public sector management and institutions."

The objectives of the study are to: (a) identify emerging PSMG issues and challenges in the countries and regions covered; (b) identify good practices around the emerging issues and challenges identified; and (c) consider pathways that ADB and its DMCs can take to respond to such issues and challenges. The expectation is that ADB and its DMCs will thus be able to achieve more meaningful development impacts.

Methodology

Whole-of-government approach. The methodology used in the analysis of the relevant macrofiscal and governance issues includes taking a systems perspective (**Box 1**), which is anchored on a whole-of-government approach to looking at issues in PSMG.

Box 1. Systems Perspective on Macrofiscal and Governance Considerations

The focus on a systems perspective is very important in discussing macrofiscal and governance considerations, particularly as governments move away from a unidimensional and parochial way of looking at reforms.

A whole-of-government approach is needed to: (a) ensure coordinated work, (b) enhance policy coherence, (c) account for trade-offs, and (d) effectuate joined-up governance for service delivery enhancements. The end result of a whole-of-government approach is to get a better handle on unintended consequences of public policies.

Source: J. Low. 2016. Singapore's Whole-of-Government Approach in Crisis Management. Ethos. Civil Service College, Singapore.

PSMG country diagnostics. Recognizing the need for flexible and country-specific approaches that raise the quality of macrofiscal and governance frameworks in its DMCs, ADB conducts country diagnostic assessments as part of its country partnership strategy (CPS) preparation with each of its DMCs. The diagnostic exercises enable the formulation of proposed measures to strengthen related legal and regulatory frameworks, institutions, and capacities with concrete inputs for the CPS. It also supports the identification of policy-based reform programs, reform areas, and specific policy actions that will strengthen country systems and the enabling environment for effective development outcomes in each DMC. The study leverages information generated from these assessments as it analyses varied governance and operating environments across the region.

Use of CPA evidence. ADB conducts a biennial CPA exercise for all DMCs that have access to concessional resources. Assessment is based on: (a) the quality of macroeconomic management; (b) the coherence of structural policies; (c) the degree to which policies and institutions promote equity and inclusion; (d) the quality of PSMG; and (e) the performance of the concessional assistance project portfolio. The CPA exercise results consist of scores in four clusters of variables,[6] of which those in Cluster D (on governance) are the most relevant for this study.

6 The four clusters are: (1) *Cluster A (on Economic Management)* – (a) Monetary and exchange rate policies; (b) Fiscal policy; and (c) Debt policy and management; (2) *Cluster B (on Structural Policies)* – (a) Trade; (b) Financial sector; and (c) Business regulatory environment; (3) *Cluster C (on Policies for Social Inclusion/Equity)* – (a) Gender equity; (b) Equity of public resource use; (c) Building human resources; (d) Social protection and labor; and (e) Policies and institutions for environmental sustainability; and (4) *Cluster D (on Governance)* – (a) Property rights and rule-based governance; (b) Quality of budgetary and financial management; (c) Efficiency of revenue mobilization; (d) Quality of public administration; and (e) Transparency, accountability, and corruption in the public sector.

Concept of frontier DMCs. Drawing from the CPA, as well as other literature, the study uses frontier economies as benchmarks, for example, Georgia, on fiscal transparency based on the 2023 Open Budget Survey[7] where it is ranked first among 125 countries assessed across the world. For purposes of specific focus on governance, and its various components, Bhutan is regarded as a good frontier DMC because: (a) its governance system is relatively strong, with well-established institutions, policies, processes, and arrangements; (b) the most recent (i.e., 2022) Public Expenditure and Financial Accountability (PEFA) assessment confirms that its public financial management (PFM) system is aligned with international best practices on several aspects; and (c) according to scores in the Transparency International's Corruption Perceptions Index, is consistently the ***fifth least-corrupt country*** in the entire the Asia and Pacific region (after countries such as Singapore and New Zealand, and even better than Japan in the 2024 ranking).[8] In that sense, it is a very appropriate regional frontier comparator. Where good practices in other DMCs have also been cited, this study makes references to them as well.

Evidence. The sources of evidence for this study come from:

(a) ADB's internal analytical work, due diligence, and country diagnostic assessments undertaken during the preparation of the CPS.
(b) Diagnostics work carried out for the preparation of various ADB programs/projects in DMCs.
(c) Supplementary analytical work carried out in preparation of resource allocations, such as the CPA work to determine the allocation formula for concessionary resources.
(d) Knowledge work from ADB, both institutional ones such as the Asian Development Outlook, and theme- and sector-specific studies, for example, on climate change, gender equality, and financial sector development.
(e) External reports that are referenced for analyses on governance, macrofiscal considerations, and general macroeconomic features, such as the World Development Report, and the International Monetary Fund's (IMF) Article IV consultation reports.
(f) Assessment reports, such as those centered on PEFA and public investment management (PIM).
(g) Discussions at the inaugural Workshop on Emerging Governance and Macrofiscal Issues and Opportunities, organized by the Public Sector Management and Governance Sector Office at ADB.[9]
(h) Literature review on issues in governance and PFM, both from institutional sources (such as World Bank and IMF) and from individual countries.
(i) Topical analyses in the media with respect to individual DMCs, to better capture the local context of the issues being discussed.

Caveats. There are several caveats to note in this report: (a) this is not an academic or a theoretical knowledge product, and the breadth of coverage (i.e., 34 diverse countries with varied geopolitical, social, and economic characteristics) means that the report is bound to sacrifice depth for breadth; (b) the evidence is also largely captured from ADB's internal analytical work, which means that it is carried out within certain parameters although efforts are made to triangulate the information by referring to publications and sources of evidence in the DMCs themselves; and (c) given the scope of coverage, issues are often analyzed at a broad and macro level that captures/highlights their main essence alone; more in-depth research and analysis is needed to better bring out their granularity.

[7] International Budget Partnership. Open Budget Survey (accessed 27 January 2026).
[8] Transparency International. 2024. Corruption Perceptions Index 2024 Results and Trends (accessed 27 January 2026).
[9] September 2025, Manila; conclusions from the workshop are reflected as key issues at the end of the discussions on individual topics in this study.

Key Terms and Definitions, Briefly

Governance.[10] The concept simply refers to the process of managing the affairs of the state, by which governments make rules, enforce, modify, regulate, and implement them.[11] Key dimensions of interest here are: (a) formulation and development of public policies; (b) allocation and management of resources to give effect to the public policies so developed; (c) answerability for processes followed and results attained (or not); and (d) respect for institutions that govern and that also regulate.

An associated concept is *malgovernance*. This is an overarching concept that implies an absence of good governance, thus encompassing, for example, mismanagement of resources, leakages, gaps, and unethical practices in the public sphere. In that sense, it also refers to acts of corruption and unethical practices.

Public sector management (PSM). PSM refers to the process by which agencies in the public and semi-public sectors, and at all levels (i.e., central, provincial, and local) undertake the various functions mandated of them by law and/or administrative orders. Basically, it is what public sector agencies do in order to run the affairs of the state. PSM is generally taken to be a subset of the overall concept of governance.

Governance and macrofiscal pillars (GMaPs). In addressing the complexity of country systems, the broad PSMG domain can be categorized into three GMaPs that each cover the major thematic components of a country's governance and macrofiscal frameworks: (a) domestic resource mobilization (DRM) and debt management; (b) public financial and expenditure management; and (c) oversight and accountability mechanisms. The three pillars, which also constitute the scope of ADB's PSMG country diagnostics, are discussed in Part B.

Institutions. Institutions refer to organizations that operate in the domain of the public sector and are also understood as "rules of the game" in an economic setting.[12] That strong institutions are critical for economic growth and attainment of development objectives has now been well accepted. The Asian Development Outlook states clearly the centrality of good institutions in strengthening innovation, human capital, and infrastructure development (the three pillars of productivity growth) in DMCs.[13]

Use of country systems.[14] ADB's 2015 corporate policy paper on use of country systems states that the "areas of country systems that are considered central to achieving sustainable development impact are procurement, PFM, and environmental and social (involuntary resettlement and indigenous peoples) safeguards."[15] Although this definition only covers the PFM and procurement aspects of PSMG, it should be noted that the 2015 paper

---

10 Definitions of governance (including *malgovernace*) and public sector management are taken from Bhatta. 2020. *'Those that Fix the Lights': The Practice of Public Sector Management in Developing Asia*. ADB, ADBI, and Routledge; with permission of Taylor and Francis Group.

11 At a broader level, ADB's CPA exercise specifies these components of governance: (a) property rights and rules-based governance; (b) quality of budgetary and financial management; (c) efficiency of revenue mobilization; (d) quality of public administration; and (e) transparency, accountability, and corruption in the public sector. For purposes of this study, the hierarchy of terms, at a basic level, can be seen schematically as follows: Governance encompasses PSM a component of which is PFM (which includes procurement). This structure of the narrative is contextualized later in the relevant sections of the study.

12 For a concise discussion on the meaning of the term "institutions," see, for example, Tanzi (1997). Even as they are a bit dated, the ideas therein continue to resonate with practitioners on the significant role of public sector institutions in promoting economic growth with stability and contributing to the achievement of the countries' development goals.

13 ADB. 2017a. *Asian Development Outlook 2017: Transcending the Middle-Income Challenge*. p. xi.

14 The concept of use of country systems originated at the 2005 Paris Declaration agreement among donors and partner governments on the principles of aid effectiveness (including ownership, alignment, harmonization, results management, and mutual accountability). Both multilateral and bilateral aid institutions have continued to push for the use of country systems; Department of Foreign Affairs & Trade. 2019. *Assessing and Using Partner Government Systems for Public Financial Management and Procurement: Guideline*.

15 ADB. 2015. *Promoting the Use of Country Systems in ADB's Operations: A Systematic Approach*.

only focuses on national, subnational, or sectoral systems that are considered central to achieving sustainable development impact of externally financed projects. In this sense, the principle expressed in the 2015 paper is that the strengthening of national arrangements and procedures for PFM (budgeting, treasury, accounting, auditing, and reporting) and procurement[16] will support the following outcomes: (a) reduced delays in project implementation; (b) rationalized transaction costs; (c) improved country ownership; and (d) strengthened institutions and systems of DMCs to improve service delivery and achieve sustainable development. While this approach is certainly valid at an operations level, a whole-of-government approach toward strengthening country systems requires a more holistic perspective that equally encompasses all components of the GMaP, that is, from debt management and DRM, to development planning and budget execution, to oversight mechanisms.

Public financial management (PFM). A subset of PSM, this concept refers to the budget process in a country, and can be seen along two dimensions: (a) *budget planning*, including strategic planning, revenue and expenditure forecasting, revenue mobilization, and the annual budgeting exercise; and (b) *budget execution*, including disbursements (i.e., spending or expenditure), treasury system operations, procurement, accounting, reporting, and auditing. A good PFM system will help achieve the government's policy objectives (such as improved service delivery) in a way that manages the country's resources in an effective manner (i.e., with fiscal discipline). Its contribution, however, is subject to variables such as political and bureaucratic commitment, the robustness of management information systems, and control over mismanagement of resources in the public sector. Finally, PFM issues are more or less similar at all levels of government, although the difficulties of instituting effective PFM systems at subnational levels have generally tended to be more pronounced.

Macrofiscal functions. The four components of the macrofiscal functions are: (a) macroeconomic and fiscal modeling, forecasting, and debt sustainability analysis; (b) macrofiscal policy analysis; (c) fiscal risk analysis; and (d) monitoring macroeconomic and fiscal developments.[17] Governments are expected to ensure that in the proper management of public resources, they have demonstrated due regard to value-for-money public spending, a fair and efficient tax system, and emphasized transparency and accountability in their resource use. All these are contained in the sphere of macrofiscal functions.

Strategy 2030, Its Midterm Review, and ADB's Work on Governance

The environment in which development work is taking place now in the region can be said to be characterized by many trends that impinge on what governments need to do to not only address the opportunities that arise but also manage the challenges and risks that are associated with them. For example, rapid technological advancements and greater integration to the global value chain may have provided rising opportunities for growth, but these have come with challenges as well. Rising inequality, infrastructure deficits, climate and disaster risks, and rapid urbanization, among others, continue to occupy the minds of policymakers. These realizations have been captured comprehensively in the 2024 midterm review of ADB's Strategy 2030. This review has re-energized focus in some key strategic priority areas, many of which are covered in detail in this study.

16 Procurement is considered a key component of the PFM system, but the Paris Declaration treated it separately. For purposes of this study, procurement is an integral part of the discussion on use of country systems.

17 I. Fainboim and I. Lienert. 2018. *The Macrofiscal Function and Its Organizational Arrangements*. International Monetary Fund.

In 2018, when ADB launched its Strategy 2030, the emphasis was on the unfinished development agendas in Asia and the Pacific. Its primary goal has been to focus on efforts to eradicate extreme poverty and expand its vision to achieve a prosperous, inclusive, resilient, and sustainable Asia and the Pacific. These efforts centered on, among others, (a) quality infrastructure investments that are green, sustainable, resilient, and inclusive; (b) expansion of interventions in social sectors, such as education, health, and social protection; and (c) value addition of its DMCs by combining finance, knowledge, and partnerships. Seven operational plans[18] that were in place in the initial years of the implementation of Strategy 2030 detailed how the overall objectives as stated were expected to be achieved.

The midterm review of the Strategy has coalesced ADB's critical focus on five specific areas in light of the trends and challenges the region continues to face, and it calls for accelerated action on: (a) climate action; (b) private sector development; (c) regional cooperation and public goods; (d) digital transformation; and (e) resilience and empowerment (**Figure 1**).

Figure 1. ADB's Strategic Priority Areas Pursuant to Midterm Review of Strategy 2030

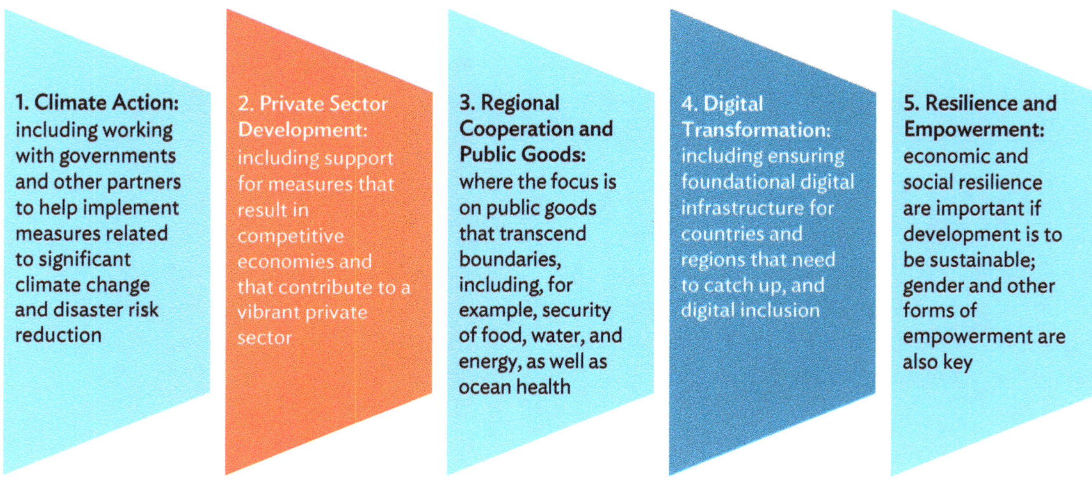

Source: ADB.

All five strategic areas documented in Figure 1 have an underlying governance focus. Governments will need to continue their attention on (a) enhanced public management and financial stability (particularly on the macroeconomic front since effective implementation of development policies hinges on strong economies and systems); (b) improved governance and institutional capacity for service delivery and for supporting private sector development; and (c) effective utilization of country systems and standards.[19]

[18] These plans were targeted in: (a) addressing and reducing inequalities; (b) accelerating gender equality; (c) tackling climate change; (d) making cities more livable; (e) promoting rural development and food security; (f) strengthening governance and capability; and (g) fostering regional cooperation.

[19] It can be argued that effective utilization of country systems is the instrument through which the first two priorities are to be achieved. This point is taken up later in this study.

Structure of the Report

This study report is structured as follows:

(a) **Part B** puts forth the basic underpinnings of the conceptual and analytical frames used in the study, including both the policy action space in governance and the stated results chain that is implicit in ADB's work in the PSMG space. This is followed by a detailed treatment of the concept of country systems since this is increasingly at the heart of how ADB currently seeks to engage with its DMCs.

(b) **Part C** provides a rather detailed treatment of the nine primary issues and challenges in macrofiscal and governance domains for the DMCs that emerge from the review of the analytical work as well as of operational portfolios of ADB. These include: (a) strengthening subnational governance; (b) enhancing domestic resource mobilization; (c) improving public financial and public expenditure systems; (d) managing fiscal risks; (e) facilitating private sector development; (f) emphasizing digitalization and service delivery; (g) focusing on climate and disaster resilience; (h) institutionalizing gender equality and social inclusion (GESI); and (a) enhancing oversight, accountability, and integrity in the public sector. It is important to mention here that these are not disparate elements, but instead need to be seen in a holistic manner, in line with the methodological imperative of a whole-of-government approach (Box 1, p. 2).

(c) The issues and challenges discussed in the previous part are then considered in **Part D** with respect to the reform pathways and opportunities for policy actions that may be considered by ADB, DMC governments, and others. Three vectors of pathways are put forth: (a) Vector 1 on systemic outcomes; (b) Vector 2 on strategic priorities; and (c) Vector 3 on instrumentation to give effect to the other two vectors of relevant elements. Part D also provides the primary conclusions that emerge from the study, with the main focus on highlighting four frames of action that help implement the opportunities highlighted in the pathways for reforms.

Several **appendixes** at the end provide further details of the various key concepts that are raised in the study.

Part B. Conceptual and Analytical Underpinnings

Policy Sphere and Concept of Information Asymmetry

The underlying approach to studying the nature of macrofiscal and governance issues and challenges needs to begin with a strong conceptual and analytical understanding of what is at the core of a government's work in the area of public policy. All things that governments undertake are anchored on public policies that are grounded on the notion of information (its availability, its access, and its usage).[20]

The notion of information and its centrality in public policy and development action, on all fronts, is anchored on the fundamental premise that there is, in reality, incomplete and imperfect information (II) in society and in the markets, which yields a situation of information asymmetry (IA) in the economy, that is, ***[II→IA]***.[21] This asymmetry impacts all aspects of economic action. Trying to minimize the information asymmetry yields ***transaction costs*** to all actors in the governance and market system; and all parties are looking for ***credible commitment*** from all others to ensure that everyone is playing by the rules. The policy claim is that governments should invest in strengthening macrofiscal and governance arrangements, which helps enhance their credible commitment to effective development action.

Table 1 exemplifies the application of the ***[II→IA]*** conceptual construct and its associated follow-through to transaction costs and credible commitment with respect to two of the five PSMG domains, as used in ADB's CPA exercise.

Results Chain

While the domain of macrofiscal and governance functions is substantial, **Figure 2** captures some of the more important facets that can help enhance the understanding of how DMCs in Asia and the Pacific have engaged to meet their overall long-term development objectives.

---

20 Joseph Stiglitz, in his Nobel Prize lecture (8 December 2001), spoke eloquently of the concept of information asymmetry and the change in the paradigm in economics. It is this concept that sits at the core of the analysis here; J. Stiglitz. 2001. Information and the Change in the Paradigm in Economics (accessed 15 July 2025).

21 See Bhatta, 2020, for detailed exposition on the relevance of the underlying relationship between incomplete information and information asymmetry with respect to governance and public sector management. Permission from Taylor & Francis Group to summarize and reproduce the core argument here is gratefully acknowledged.

Table 1. Application of Constructs with Respect to Some Public Sector Management Domains (Stylized Evidence)

Specific PSM Domain Area	*[II→IA]* Construct	Transaction Costs Incurred	Credible Commitment Demonstrated
Quality of Public Administration	Due to limited resources for translation, most laws (as well as mandated information for service delivery provisions, for example) may be in the primary language, thus constraining broader public dissemination	Lack of comprehensive customs and clearance procedures and poor quality of infrastructure are a constraint for businesses for just-in-time supply chain management, thus incurring costs to navigate the clearance system	Government approval for SOE policies that mandate rigorous reporting standards, or mandates for female representation on Boards (such as in Indonesia)
Transparency, Accountability, and Corruption in the Public Sector	Information on contract awards for procurement not made public (thus limiting transparency on the inefficiencies of not adhering to the competition principle of public procurement)	NGOs do not have ready and complete access to information on for example, procurement at local level; this increases the risks of malgovernance, as well as of their costs to carry out their mandates	Actionable decisions taken by governments to give free access to all the laws and regulations in place; or to provide access to assumptions used in revenue forecasts

IA = information asymmetry, II = imperfect information, NGO = nongovernment organization, PSM = public sector management, SOE = state-owned enterprise.

Source: Adapted from G. Bhatta. 2020.*'Those that fix the lights'...: The Practice of Public Sector Management in Developing Asia*. Routledge. Table II.1, pp. 38–39. Reproduced by permission of Taylor & Francis Group.

Figure 2. Stylized Results Chain Implicit in ADB's Work on Public Sector Management and Governance

Vision	Long term (Mongolia 2050, Viet Nam 2045); SDGs; ADB's vision of an Asia and Pacific region that is prosperous, inclusive, resilient, and sustainable			
	Strengthened country systems; improved governance and PSM; greater macrofiscal stability			
Systemic Outcomes (*Pathways*)	**1. Domestic Resource Mobilization and Debt Management**	**2. Public Financial and Expenditure Management**	**3. Oversight and accountability mechanisms**	**Overarching Domains**
Key Strategic Priorities	• Medium-term strategy • Revenue policy • Revenue administration measures – management of risks, investigation and audit, arrears monitoring • Int'l tax cooperation • Other ways to mobilize • Debt strategy, including of local governments • Debt management plan	• Fiscal strategy • Budget preparation and control • Management of fiscal risks • Treasury single account • Control of expenditure arrears • Integrity of financial information • Internal controls and audit • Public investment management • Public procurement – legal and regulatory framework, market operations, transparency, etc.	• Fiscal transparency • Monitoring of SOEs and subnational governments • Work of independent supreme audit institution • Legislative scrutiny • Accountability – of process, use of resources, and results • Anticorruption mechanisms • Oversight and ethics: roles of Legislature, regulators, CSOs	• Involvement of private sector through for example, PPPs, access to credit, competition policy, SOE reforms, etc. • Infrastructure governance • Inclusiveness, transparency • Subnational governance • Credible commitment to legal and policy systems • Capacity development • Climate and disaster resilience
Instrument-ation	• Digitalization and information systems • Access to information legislative arrangements • CSO engagement • Adherence to global standards (e.g., ISA, BEPS, AML/CFT) • Move towards a National Integrity Strategy • Accreditation of those in the procurement profession (e.g., CIPS)		• Gender responsive budgeting • Intersectionality of themes (e.g., CDR in infrastructure governance) • MTFF, MTBF, Fiscal Rules • Use of analytical tools: such as PEFA, PIMA, and TADAT • M and E protocols, including social safeguards • Risk portfolio management, for example, contingent liabilities	

ADB = Asian Development Bank; AML/CFT = anti-money laundering and combating the financing of terrorism; BEPS = base erosion and profit shifting; CDR = climate and disaster resilience; CIPS = Chartered Institute of Procurement & Supply; CSOs = civil society organizations; ISA = International Standards on Auditing; M&E = monitoring and evaluation; MTBF = medium-term budgetary framework; MTFF = medium-term fiscal framework; PEFA = public expenditure and financial accountability; PIMA = public investment management assessment; PPPs = public–private partnerships; PSM = public sector management; SDGs = Sustainable Development Goals; SOEs = state-owned enterprises; TADAT = tax administration diagnostic assessment tool.

Source: Authors; loosely adapted from ADB's Operational Plan 6 on Governance and Institution Building for Strategy 2030.

Figure 2 is specific to the realms covered in this study and proceeds as follows:

(a) Attainment of development visions and objectives is a function of improved governance and PSM, strengthened country systems, and greater macrofiscal stability.
(b) These result from the systemic outcomes (or pathways) evident in DRM and debt management, public financial and expenditure management, and oversight and accountability mechanisms.
(c) Key strategic priorities in these three outcomes are numerous and include, for example, prudent debt policies and strategies, well-thought through DRM measures (that are centered on taxes primarily but go much beyond that), proper management of fiscal risks, strong internal controls and audits, a sound public procurement greater fiscal transparency, aggressive legislative scrutiny, and strong focus on accountability mechanisms.
(d) Overarching domains within which these systems operate include, among others, involvement of the private sector, subnational governance, infrastructure governance, focus on inclusiveness and transparency, credible commitment of governments to the laws and their own stated policies, and capacity development measures throughout.
(e) Finally, governments have at their disposal various instruments to realize their strategic priorities; these include digitalization, civil society organization (CSO) engagement, adherence to global standards in many areas, gender-responsive budgeting, adherence to robust fiscal rules, proper use of analytical tools (e.g., PEFA and PIMA), and strong risk portfolio management measures.

Strengthening Country Systems

Historically, discussions, reports, and studies on country systems have revolved primarily around global declarations on aid effectiveness (e.g., Paris, Accra, Busan, and Mexico) and the use of such systems by providers of development finance.[22] In this context, the essence of the use of country systems involved commitments from partner countries to strengthen their national systems, and commitments from development partners to use such systems to the maximum extent possible; and the focus of PSMG-related literature on this issue revolved around the budgeting, treasury, accounting, auditing, reporting, and procurement arrangements and systems.[23]

While such historical approaches have provided a good starting point, subsequent events have exposed emerging and recurring issues that demonstrate the need for a much broader perspective of country systems, as well as a whole-of-government approach towards strengthening such systems. Among others, these events include exogenous shocks like the COVID-19 pandemic and lockdowns, the increased exposure of DMCs to risks of climate-related disasters, and political transitions and social movements in specific jurisdictions triggered by integrity-related issues. These events have not only exposed countries within the region to unprecedented fiscal risks that highlighted the importance of sound DRM and debt management policies and practices, but also revealed systemic gaps in national financial, and expenditure management systems.

22 Paris Declaration on Aid Effectiveness 2005; Accra Agenda for Action 2008; Global Partnership for Effective Development Cooperation 2011; Mexico High Level Meeting Communique 2014; Cusco Declaration on Procurement and Manila Consensus on PFM 2011; and other aid effectiveness documents. Organisation for Economic Co-operation and Development (OECD). Development Co-operation Directorate. Aid Effectiveness (accessed 27 January 2026).

23 For a concise discussion on the use of country systems, particularly from a practice perspective, see J. Syquia. 2023. What Can Be Done to Improve the Use of Country Governance Systems?. It is relevant to note here that OECD accepts that 'use of country systems' implies that it is really a continuum of practices and that donors can be engaged in this to a greater or lesser degree (i.e., it is not an 'all or nothing' proposition but at a minimum use country planning, budgeting, and reporting systems, whatever the modality and risk threshold).

Viewing Country Systems by Frames

At a more generic and conceptual level, the term country systems takes into account three sets of frames (components, enablers, and results chain) that trace the need to strengthen policy, legal, and institutional frameworks for development effectiveness (**Appendix 2**). It looks at three pillars of governance and macrofiscal functions: domestic resource mobilization and debt management, public financial and expenditure management, and oversight and accountability mechanisms. There are several items of note on the schematic representation of country systems (Appendix 2) as it applies to ADB's work in its DMCs. These include:

(a) Three distinct sets that define the structure and flow of country systems: (i) set 1: components (or pillars); (ii) set 2: enablers; and (iii) set 3: results chain.
(b) Pathways for strengthening the pillars of governance and macrofiscal (GMaP) functions.
(c) A focus on central and subnational governments (SNGs), which is a critical aspect of ADB's work and forms the core of localizing the Sustainable Development Goals (SDGs) agenda.
(d) Enablers that apply at all levels of government and cover four distinct components: (i) people (e.g., elected officials); (ii) technology (e.g., to enable real-time feedback); (iii) systems, processes, and resources (e.g., robust monitoring and evaluation systems); and (iv) structures (e.g., civil society, skills development institutions).
(e) The most critical part of the schematic description of the country system is that on results chain, which looks at how the enablers contribute to the three pillars in terms of outcome achievement –
    (i) The first is the set of five specific outcomes sought by governments: (1) effective long-term resource planning and use; (2) effective PFM and procurement systems; (3) greater fiscal stability; (4) efficient, inclusive, and accessible public service delivery; and (5) enhanced oversight and accountability mechanisms.
    (ii) The second is that the successful attainment of these outcomes, other things being equal, eventually results in increased development effectiveness, that is, a higher-level outcome attained.
    (iii) The above, in turn, leads to the attainment of national visions (however, those may have been articulated, e.g., Mongolia 2050).

Country Systems Strengthening Pathways

Based on recent experiences of ADB's diagnostic work in the preparation of the CPSs, several common yet critical weak links have been identified in the GMaP systems in DMCs.

(a) The **planning-to-budgeting gap** reflects the disconnect between national development plans and agency budgets. This is often observed when the national planning exercise is not informed by robust medium-term fiscal framework (MTFF), and is compounded when sector plans are not prepared or do not inform budgeting and planning exercises at the implementing agency level. This is an often-occurring phenomenon in DMCs and can be considered the first weak link in the system.
(b) The **budget integration gap** is evident when the capital/investment budget is not integrated with the recurrent and maintenance budget, and is often a symptom of the planning-to-budgeting gap or weak medium-term fiscal framework (MTEF).
(c) The **system integration gap,** where key aspects of a country's system are not adequately linked together, for example, the Integrated Financial Management Information System, is incomplete or has not yet been implemented.
(d) Opportunities also exist to strengthen the integration of climate-responsive and disaster resilience objectives, as well as gender and social inclusion, in national and subnational PFM systems, to address the **climate, disaster, and gender gap**. This would involve the development of national and subnational development plans that incorporate elements related to climate change adaptation or mitigation, disaster risk management, and gender and social inclusion, as well as measures to introduce/strengthen budget tagging and expenditure tracking for such areas.

(e) A **national-to-subnational gap** has also been observed, where development plans, priorities, and strategies at the national and sectoral levels are not effectively cascaded to the subnational level through well-aligned local development plans and investment plans.

To achieve a holistic approach in strengthening a country's systems, a reform pathway needs to be designed such that gaps identified above are prioritized and addressed through a sequenced set of actions that weave through all of the components of the pillars. While some reform actions will be easier to implement than others, it should be noted that any reform that is introduced in a silo will eventually be compromised by risks in other areas. For instance, the benefits of procurement reforms will not be maximized if they are not complemented by upstream reforms in the areas of planning, budgeting, and public investment management, or by reforms to strengthen external audits and oversight functions.

It is only by managing reforms across multiple fronts that governments will be able to successfully respond to economic crises and other shocks and achieve (and sustain) macrofiscal stability. A meaningful reform program needs to prioritize and sequence legal, regulatory, and institutional strengthening measures across the following pillars:

(a) *Pillar 1: DRM and debt management.* The success of a DMC in achieving the objectives of its national development strategies and the SDGs depends on its ability to mobilize financial resources and maintain sustainable levels of public debt. In turn, the ability to mobilize the needed revenue for effective development requires a broad tax base, enhanced tax compliance, and a transparent and efficient tax administration that benefits from digital technologies. Increased mobilization of domestic resources would not only reduce the need to issue domestic debt, but would also address possible overreliance on external debt, which may undermine the use of fiscal and monetary policy to support domestic economies.

    On DRM, the main areas covered by this theme are the DMC's institutional, organizational, and governance arrangements for revenue collection, tax compliance, and major compliance risks, which include aggressive tax avoidance, tax fraud, base erosion and profit shifting, and revenue collection systems and processes. With respect to debt management, the main areas covered are the DMC's debt management functions, the capacity of institutions to manage public debt effectively and sustainably, the management of contingent liabilities, which includes those arising from state-owned enterprises (SOE), and debt management reforms.

(b) *Pillar 2: Public financial and expenditure management.* Strategy 2030 Priority 6 stresses that effective PFM is central to a DMC's capability to implement its policy objectives and national development and poverty reduction plans. It is at the core of a government's ability to utilize public resources to deliver efficient and sustainable infrastructure and services. Relatedly, sound public expenditure management will help achieve impactful development outcomes by ensuring that public sector planning, budgeting, and execution benefit from aggregate fiscal discipline, allocative efficiency, and operational efficiency.

    The main topics of this pillar include the legislative, regulatory and institutional frameworks for public financial and expenditure management, the performance of relevant national ministries and agencies, budget transparency, public investment management, and recent reforms and current challenges. This pillar also includes the legislative, regulatory, and institutional frameworks for public procurement, procurement management capacity, and procurement operations and market practices.

(c) *Pillar 3: Oversight and accountability mechanisms.* The formal oversight provided by legislatures and state audit institutions (SAIs) plays a fundamental role in the public financial and expenditure management processes. CSOs can play an important role in enhancing the transparency of PFM and public expenditure management, including as independent watchdogs, but they cannot replace effective oversight institutions. Further, since good governance is characterized by accountable public institutions, governments and development partners alike have recognized the importance of fighting corruption and strengthening government accountability mechanisms.

As such, the roles of the legislature and SAIs need to be complemented by effective anticorruption institutions and programs that focus on the supply side of governance reforms. The main topics in this pillar include policy, legislative, regulatory and institutional frameworks on reporting, external audit and anticorruption, audit standards and practices, international commitments on anticorruption, and corruption perception. Another aspect that may be covered is the relationship of the state with the media and civil society.

A Focus on the Use of Country Systems

The above discussion provides the broad principles on strengthening country systems for improved macrofiscal and governance frameworks. From such broad perspectives, a narrower focus can be considered in the context of using country systems for donor-assisted projects. This narrower approach would bring us back to the six elements that the Organisation for Economic Co-operation and Development (OECD) has highlighted as key elements in the use of country system: budgeting, treasury, accounting, auditing, reporting, and procurement.[24] These components are conceptually, and functionally, closely related, as demonstrated in **Figure 3**.

Figure 3. Stylized Schematic Framework for Use of Country Systems

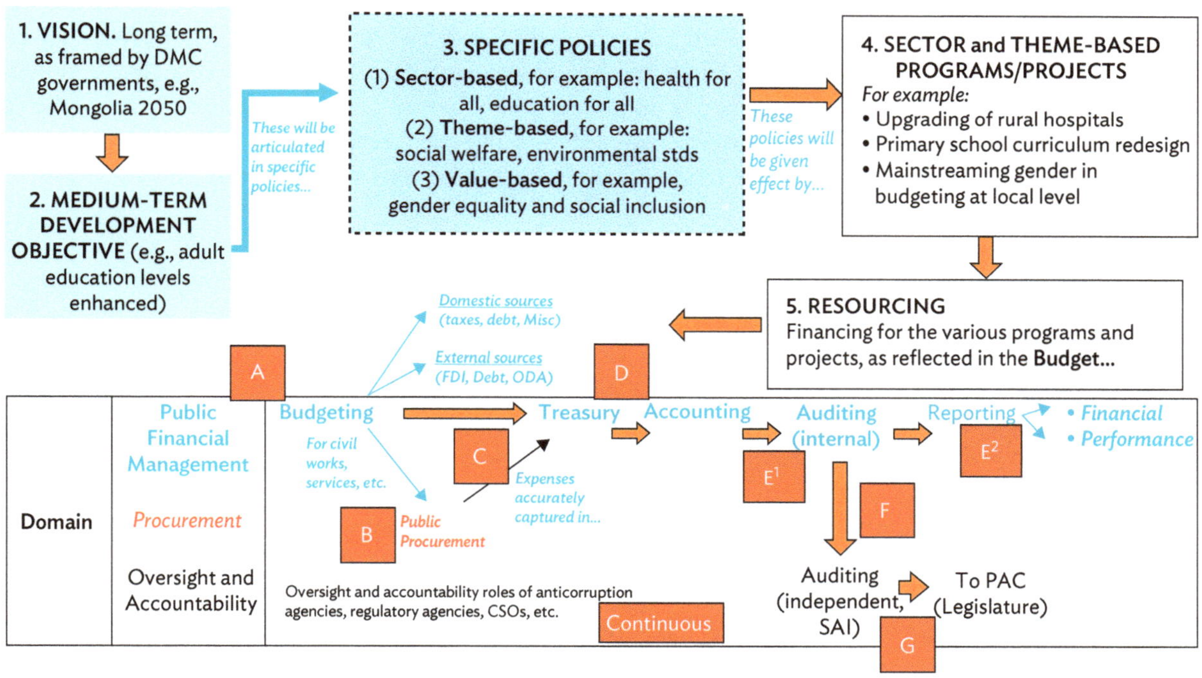

CSO = civil society organizations, DMC = developing member country, FDI = foreign direct investment, ODA = overseas development assistance, PAC = Public Accounts Committee, SAI = state audit institution.

Source: Authors.

[24] See **Appendix 3** for the decision metrics for ascertaining the degree of usage of country systems for ADB operations.

Figure 3 may look complex, but it is not, and it is important that the narrative is made clear:

(a) Narratives across 1–5:
   (i) 1 – The long-term vision of the country sets the broad framework for what the main development goals are.
   (ii) 2 – The mid-term development goals, which could be articulated, for example, in 5-year plans.
   (iii) 3 – These goals are articulated in specific sector and theme-based policies as well as what can be termed "value-based" ones, such as gender equality.
   (iv) 4 – To give effect to the goals and policies, specific programs (at sector and theme levels) are designed and implemented.
   (v) 5 – Appropriate and adequate levels of resourcing will need to be provided in order for the programs and projects to be implemented effectively. At the annual and medium-term level, this is inherent in the budgets developed by the government.

(b) Narratives across A–G: (a) governments prioritize to specific policies through resourcing decisions (i.e., **budgeting**) (see **[A]**); (b) resources from the budget are used to publicly procure services, goods, civil works, etc. from the public procurement sphere (see **[B]**); (c) both the budgetary use and procurement expenses are accurately captured in the Treasury system (see **[C]** and **[D]**); (d) which are then accounted for (see **[D]**) to ensure that all the resource usage is effectively and accurately captured; (e) these accounts need to be audited both internally (see **[E1]**) and externally (i.e., independently) (see **[F]**); (f) reporting done by agencies (see **[E2]**) for the use of funds is inherent in financial and performance-related information that is publicly presented; (g) the reporting done by the independent supreme audit institution (see **[G]**) that carries out the independent scrutiny is submitted to the legislature; and (h) as part of the oversight and accountability measures, the roles of anticorruption agencies, regulatory agencies, and CSOs are on an ongoing (see **[Continuous]**) basis.

Measures to strengthen country systems should come hand-in-hand with development partners' reliance on such systems, particularly when these result in improved legal and institutional frameworks, efficient processes, and stronger capacities and institutions. OECD and other international organizations have argued that, in turn, the use of country systems can provide incentives and momentum to strengthen the capacity and performance of developing countries, enhance domestic accountability mechanisms, and improve the effectiveness of public expenditure, regardless of the source of financing (i.e., whether from the national budget or from development assistance).

An analysis of ADB's own country diagnostics and programs, as well as experiences of other development partners, reveals the following interesting points with respect to the use of country systems:

(a) Development partners have made greater headway in the use of country systems for planning and budgeting purposes. Such a situation demonstrates that the partner concerned effectively integrates its development assistance programs with the government's national planning and budgeting processes, thus increasing the country's ownership of such programs and their outcomes.
(b) Development partners also tend to rely on national accounting, reporting, and treasury systems, especially when a treasury single account (TSA) exists. Along with national planning and budgeting systems, the accounting, reporting, and treasury components of a country's system have been highlighted by OECD as minimum-use requirements. According to the OECD, these components promote a level of transparency that is essential for country ownership of overseas development assistance (ODA), alignment of aid, donor harmonization, managing for results, and mutual accountability.[25]

[25] OECD. 2011. *Using Country Public Financial Management Systems: A Practitioner's Guide.* p. 24.

Box 2. Use of Multilateral Development Bank vs. Country Procurement Systems

In the World Bank's 2014 evaluation of its use of country procurement systems, it reported that the area of contention was not necessarily the systems of multilateral development banks (MDBs) versus country systems, but rather the advantages of using MDBs' systems, with the concomitant benefits of experience and transparency.

To be more precise, the evaluation found that contractors and suppliers clearly favored the use of the World Bank's procurement systems over country systems because they perceived these as having embedded safeguards that help maintain equal opportunities, greater transparency and assurances of integrity, more efficient payment systems, and effective recourse in cases of complaints.

Sources: World Bank. 2014. *The World Bank Group and Public Procurement: An Independent Evaluation.* p. 18; and World Bank. 2014. *The World Bank and Public Procurement – An Independent Evaluation. Volume II: Achieving Development Effectiveness through Procurement in Bank Financial Assistance.* p. 28.

(c) Despite the extent of procurement reforms across developing countries development partners do not seem to be relying extensively and consistently on national procurement systems. As evident in **Box 2**, this may be related to observations that integrity risks tend to increase as one progresses from the planning and budgeting stages of the PFM process toward the procurement and expenditure stages, primarily because of the increasing interaction between the government and the private sector (e.g., during public biddings). In any case, it needs to be borne in mind that integrity risks also exist in the upstream stages of the PFM cycle, such as when unjustified line items are inserted during the preparation of the national budget. Such a risk may exist when planning and budgeting processes lack transparency or suffer from systemic gaps, or when oversight functions are compromised, and are eventually linked to corrupted procurement practices.

(d) The main fiduciary safeguard applied for MDB-financed projects that do not use country systems is establishing project management units to administer and oversee project implementation. Action plans can be prepared to address identified governance weaknesses of executing and implementing agencies for each project, but the project management units have the effect of ring-fencing the project.

(e) In all elements of the country systems for PFM and procurement, robust information management systems (e.g., an integrated financial management information system) and their proper applications are a must. Where the use of country systems is partial or not evident at all, it is partly a function of the absence of such information systems.

(f) Selected DMCs' adherence to, and institutionalization of, global standards (such as the International Public Sector Accounting Standards [IPSAS]) demonstrates their credible commitment to strengthening country systems.

(g) There is uniformly considerable evidence on misappropriations, losses, and other lapses in the proper use of government resources in the reports of external audit bodies (e.g., the Commission on Audit (COA) in the Philippines). Since the legislatures review these, they serve as meaningful knowledge sources and evidentiary bases for assessing governance lapses.

Some Key Issues to Note on Practice of Country Systems

Reforms that are low-hanging fruit. The danger of focusing on low-hanging fruits can be viewed from two angles: (a) that the government initiates reforms only on easy aspects of the problem (and does not leverage the momentum generated); and (b) it is, all too often, easier to reform in isolation (or a stand-alone manner) than to target the issue in an integrated manner. It is this component of integrated policy reforms that features prominently in all discussions on PSMG reforms.

Use of country systems vs. strength of country systems. A critical distinction is made between using country systems (i.e., development partners relying on them for projects) and the inherent strength of those systems. The argument is that when development partners use country systems, they strengthen them by exposing government agencies to international standards, thereby enhancing domestic accountability and improving the quality of PFM. In practice, the use of country systems has not really moved as much – on average, only 50% of development financing uses country systems. One plausible reason is that non-technical causes, such as political considerations, governance concerns, or reputational risks, often play a significant role in their non-use.

Stakeholder perspectives and trust. The perception of country systems by key stakeholders – particularly the private sector and civil society – is a crucial indicator of their effectiveness. For example, the private sector has generally less confidence in the transparency and accountability of country systems, especially in procurement and payments. Further, CSOs are often seen as antagonists of governments when it comes to areas such as procurement although there is potential for beneficial engagement between the two, beyond procurement and into such areas as participatory planning, budgeting, and auditing.

Challenges in prioritizing reforms. Identifying and sequencing priority reforms remains a foundational challenge for governments as they seek to improve aggregate fiscal discipline, allocative efficiency, and operational efficiency. There is generally a spectrum of pressing issues, from refining foundational transactional processes to addressing systemic disconnects across governments, each underscoring the complex and multifaceted nature of public financial and expenditure management modernization.

Public financial and expenditure management reforms cannot succeed in a vacuum. To be truly effective, they must serve as a vehicle for advancing broader national development priorities. Critical agendas such as climate change, disaster risk management, and gender equality should not be treated as stand-alone initiatives or sectoral afterthoughts. Instead, they must be fundamentally integrated into core processes, including planning, budgeting, and expenditure tracking, to ensure that policy commitments translate into tangible and measurable outcomes. Technical and process-oriented reforms, while essential, derive their ultimate value from the governance frameworks that ensure they are implemented transparently and with full accountability to the public.

Part C. Emerging Issues and Challenges in Macrofiscal and Governance Domains

A review of the literature, prior and ongoing analytical work of ADB, CPS preparation country diagnostic work, and other knowledge work shows several issues and challenges in the public space being highlighted; these can be generally categorized as follows (see **Figure 4**):

Figure 4. Key Issues Inherent in the Practice of Public Sector Management and Governance in Developing Member Countries

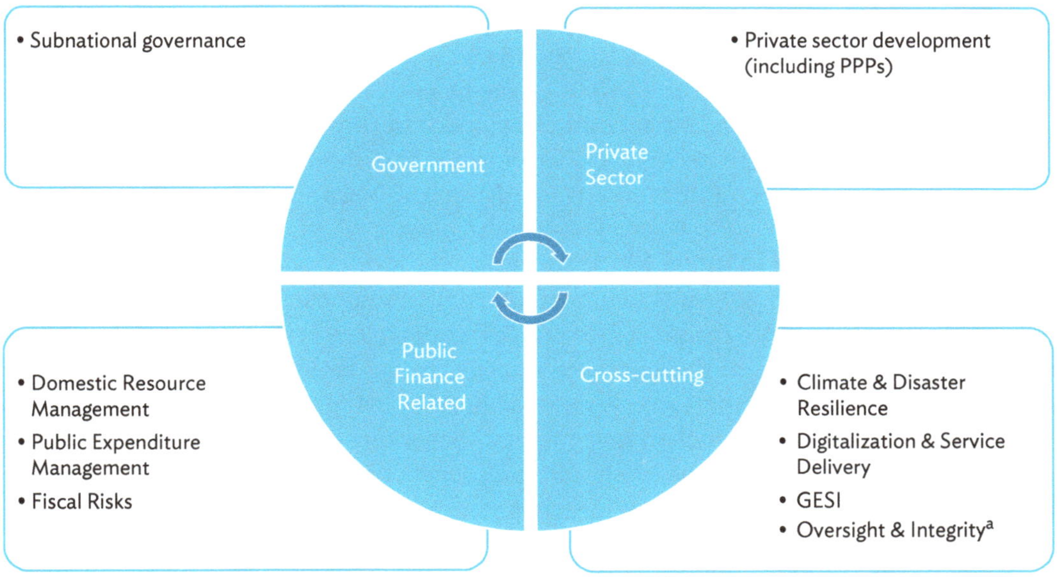

GESI = gender equality and social inclusion, PPP = public–private partnerships.

Notes:

[a] While the standard terminology used is oversight and accountability, this study employs the concept of "integrity" to elevate and broaden the conversation on accountability. After all, accountability is already presumed inherent in the oversight functions. A focus on integrity enables Developing Member Countries to have a different narrative on governance that enables them to introduce the focus on actions on the ground that embed the practice of ethics in all matters related to Public Sector Management and Governance. This is also in line with the methodological specification of a whole-of-government approach that sits at the core of the review work in this study.

Source: Authors.

Strengthening Subnational Governance[26]

The focus of SDG Goal 16, particularly on "effective, accountable, and inclusive institutions at all levels" is relevant to the theme of strengthening subnational governance. It signifies that subnational governments play a critical and direct role in impacting the everyday lives of citizens.

At the heart of the relevance of subnational governance in terms of the focus of this study are three elements: (a) localizing the global development agenda, anchored on the SDGs; (b) ensuring a strong link among local governance, service delivery, PFM issues, and accountability from a political and political economy perspective; and (c) prioritizing service delivery enhancements, which is ultimately the function of governments.

Localizing the Global Agenda

The aspect of localization of the global agenda takes into account subnational political and development contexts, as reflected in: (a) awareness-raising of the SDGs, and their implications for local action across SNG entities, CSOs, and the public; (b) incorporating subnational views and aspirations into the national sustainable development strategies; and (c) empowering SNGs to carry out development actions in line with SDG aspirations.

Localizing the development agenda has to be considered in light of the nature of subnational governance. In Nepal, for example, where a federal form of government is in place, spatial units have a greater degree of political autonomy with their own executive, legislative, and judicial arrangements within the federal republic system. In contrast, in the Lao People's Democratic Republic (Lao PDR), the government's decentralization policy (known as the *Sam Sang Policy*) has three elements: a political manifesto, an approach to decentralized administration, and a national targeted development program. In this regard, the 17 provinces are assigned as strategic units, the 149 districts as responsible for planning and budget preparation, and more than 8,500 villages as development units.

Strengthening Local Public Financial Management

Mirroring the efforts of central governments to ensure robust PFM systems, SNGs also seek to strengthen their local systems so that these align with the same PFM principles adopted by central governments. Different DMCs have different needs in this regard. In Cambodia, for example, recent efforts to advance decentralization have included strengthening a unified internal control system across the central government and line ministries/SNGs. Nepal, on the other hand, is more focused on streamlining and making its intergovernmental fiscal arrangements fit-for-purpose, such that the (relatively) newly formed subnational entities (i.e., the seven provinces, and 753 municipalities) can carry out their mandated functions more effectively, and with more confidence on resource flows and provisions.

As the case of Nepal amply demonstrates, SNGs seek predictability and credibility in central government resources and fund flows, which in turn improve how they manage their own PFM systems. This is largely because SNGs tend to rely significantly on the national government for their resourcing. To avoid a fiscal crisis, SNGs are strengthening their own public sector institutions, particularly as the legal provisions on intergovernmental fiscal transfers give them substantial control over such institutions.[27]

---

26 For an analysis of central and local government relations, particularly as they relate to fiscal sustainability in Asia, see, for example, Morgan and Trinh, 2017; and OECD and ADB, 2023.

27 For an analysis of the relevant issues of subnational fiscal crises and how to address them, see, for example, Nakatani, 2025.

Focusing on Subnational Governance for Service Delivery Enhancements

Strengthening local governance for enhanced public service delivery is the crux of the subject matter in this section.[28] The clear focus of service delivery enhancements as part of stronger subnational governance is evident in several dimensions; **Table 2** illustrates this conceptual framing and serves as a useful approach for analyzing subnational governance.

Table 2. Local Governance and Service Delivery—An Approach to Analysis

Domains	Actions	Example(s) of Conduits
Stated and revealed preferences	Citizen-clients make preferences known, which are then debated, and agreed upon, in line with mandated provisions and systems	• Through market behavior • Through negotiations between the executive body (e.g., municipal government) and legislature (e.g., municipal council)
Scale of demand and formal approval	Local governments aggregate the preferences to determine which ones to finance at what level, and secure approval at local council level	• Check for consistency with nationally set goals and mandates (part of the process of localizing global development agenda) • Check for financial congruence (i.e., in line with locally generated budgets, own-source revenue)
Regulatory framework	Development of the frameworks that are both products of allowable provisions under the Constitution as well as inherent in intergovernmental fiscal frameworks	• Regulatory provisions that are mandated from the center (e.g., on oversight mechanisms related to financial control of resources transferred from the center) • By-laws, for example, passed by the local councils that permit municipal governments to carry out their regulatory functions
Service delivery	Public services delivered to the standards that SNGs themselves will have detailed, as well as those that will have been mandated from the center	• Through executive agencies at local level • Through contracts with the private sector; contract management processes will have been agreed upon by both parties • Now increasingly through civil society and community groups
Relationship with central government	At all spheres of governance, including: (a) political, (b) fiscal, and (c) social	• Political: subnational governance as per the Constitution • Fiscal: Expenditure and revenue assignments • Social: GESI provisions in local bodies aligned with national policy
Subnational PFM	• The application of central systems at the subnational level, and the development of subnational systems developed for local governance and fiscal management • Fiscal provisions, such as on internal loans for revenue generation	• Integrated to the Financial Management Information System of the central government • Local Government Management Information System • Budgeting, accounting, reporting, and internal controls in subnational level agencies (but aligned, where mandated, to central systems) • Provisions for SNGs to borrow internally, to the level mandated by relevant laws
Monitoring	• Delivery and monitoring of public services • Corrections made if *ex-ante* and *ex-post* variance is evident or progress is slow	• Through internal control entities of executive agencies • Through civil society → for example, citizen score cards • Through regular planning and budget channels • Through citizen-oriented social accountability mechanisms
Audits and evaluation	Regular audits of performance and results, including financial management	• Through watchdog agencies (such as Office of Auditor General or delegated entity) • Through civil society → social audits

GESI = gender equality and social inclusion, PFM = public financial management, SNG = subnational government.

Source: Adapted from G. Bhatta. 2020. *'Those that fix the lights'...: The Practice of Public Sector Management in Developing Asia*. Routledge. Table 10.1, p. 182. Reproduced by permission of Taylor & Francis Group.

28 The term "service delivery" refers to the actions of governments (central, provincial, and local) in providing public services to citizens. Such services can be of many types: (a) infrastructural, such as transport, energy; (b) social, such as education; (c) regulatory, such as licensing; and (d) emergency, such as rescue during disasters due to natural hazards (see A. Deolalikar, S. Jha, and P. Quising, eds. 2015. *Governance in Developing Asia: Public Service Delivery and Empowerment*. p. 3).

Underlying the policy narrative on service delivery enhancements is the fact that "governance is... at the core of service delivery problems" and that "the challenge is to improve the quality of public services."[29] Indeed, when it comes to the assessment of decentralization, the extension of successful government performance often veers to the metric of service delivery enhancement. In this regard, it is instructive to see Indonesia's efforts to improve the quality of fiscal transfers and SNG spending for service delivery.

Examples from Indonesia and Nepal

Indonesia has had some of the most significant subnational governance experiences to date. The Big Bang of fiscal decentralization (anchored on the enactment of two key laws – Law No. 11/1999 on regional government, and Law No. 5/1999 on financial balance between central and regional governments) meant considerable regional autonomy with delegated powers to regions to manage their fiscal budgets, both in terms of revenues and expenditures.[30] This also meant SNGs (i.e., provinces, districts, and villages) manage the delivery of most key services at local level.

ADB's analysis of subnational governance in Indonesia identifies two gaps that can contextualize the way one understands the nature of equity, accountability, and PFM institutions affecting service access and quality at local level:

(a) *Accountability gap*. Districts currently lack strong accountability for improving the quality of public service spending due to issues such as lack of effective monitoring by central government of districts' spending performance.

(b) *PFM institutions gap*. Local leaders are not fully supported to make informed spending decisions due to, for example, a disconnect between districts' budgets and local budget reliability. Also, internal controls at the local level are generally weak.

One specific approach that may be considered is the fiscal interest model,[31] which inherently supports a hard budget constraint on local governments for use of the transferred funds, requiring them to face the full financial consequences of their spending decisions.[32] As a newly federated country (since 2015, following more than two centuries of monarchical rule), Nepal offers recent lessons on issues of subnational governance. **Box 3** articulates relevant issues in Nepal, particularly with respect to fiscal governance at local level.

Issues of Credible Commitment with Respect to Resourcing

Credible commitment in fiscal decentralization generally tends to be low in systems where central and local governments have severe capacity constraints, and where mechanisms to discuss both sets of interests (such as a joint forum) are absent or ineffective. Confidence-building measures are critical in this regard, especially where inherent biases are embedded in the system. For example, SNGs tend to provide incomplete information to the national government, or the central government tends to justify delays in the release of funds to local governments.[33]

[29] A. Deolalikar, S. Jha, and P. Quising, eds. 2015. *Governance in Developing Asia: Public Service Delivery and Empowerment*. p. 152.

[30] Government of Indonesia and USAID. 2021. *Two Decades of Fiscal Decentralization Implementation in Indonesia*.

[31] B. Weingast. 2009. Second Generation Fiscal Federalism: The Implications of Fiscal Incentives. *Journal of Urban Economics*. 65(3). pp. 279–293.

[32] In this regard, there is literature (see e.g., Qian and Roland, 1998) that shows that local governments will be more inefficient if they face soft rather than hard budget constraints. Soft budget constraints can also be provided at institutional level; for example, in Cambodia, line ministries are guided by a Circular on Annual Budget Preparation where the ceilings provided for current and capital expenditures are only at the sector level, and only indicative soft ceilings are given for recurrent expenditures.

[33] For a comprehensive review of the issues centered on fiscal decentralization in many countries of developing Asia, see, for example, Yoshino and Morgan, eds, 2017.

Box 3. Issues in Subnational Fiscal Governance—Lessons from Nepal

1. Despite only moving to a federal form of government in 2015, Nepal has, by all accounts, made considerable progress on subnational public financial management performance. The seven provinces have established planning commissions and prepared periodic development plans as well as MTEF. However, most of the 753 local governments have not done so, largely due to lack of capacity and skills.
2. Substantial overlaps, duplications, and ambiguities continue to exist in the intergovernmental framework of operations and pose a challenge in subnational governments. Detailing and unbundling of the functions, functionaries, and finances by the federal government has been protracted and is yet to be completed.
3. The central government is committed to consolidation measures, including expenditure rationalization, by reducing administrative and non-essential recurrent spending, and lowering fiscal transfers to subnational governments (by focusing on programs that have not been progressing efficiently). Subnational governments underspend their annual budgets regularly even as their own source revenue mobilization is much lower than the optimal level.
4. There are still concerns over expenditure and revenue assignments, particularly between the Center and subnational governments. This situation has not been helped by an absence of relevant institutional structures and processes across many domains (e.g., despite the Inter-Governmental Fiscal Management Act being enacted in 2016, a decade later there are still no applicable regulations developed to give effect to the provisions of the Act, which effectively means, for example, that subnational governments have not been able to take recourse to generating internal loans to augment their resource mobilization).
5. There is still no federal enabling framework law in many other areas (that is being considered and will facilitate subnational governments to develop their own laws based upon this) such as on education, police, civil service, etc., where the lack of federal law has constrained subnational level governance action.

Source: Country diagnostic work for the Nepal CPS, 2024; see also Bhatta, 2021.

One specific aspect of credible commitment that influences the performance ecosystem of both subnational and national governments has to do with resourcing (of all types, but particularly financial). Thus, resource mobilization, specifically from domestic sources, has been highlighted significantly since 2015 (with the Addis Ababa Action Agenda adopted at the 3rd International Conference on Financing for Development); this issue of DRM is discussed later.

Some Key Issues to Note in Subnational Governance

Systemic disconnect: aligning plans, projects, and budgets. The strategic alignment of planning, project pipelines, and budgetary allocations is the bedrock of effective PFM and responsive service delivery. When these elements are disconnected, public resources are misallocated, development priorities remain unfunded, and accountability is obscured. This issue of systemic disconnection appears evident across developing countries, and is a multifaceted one rooted in structural, operational, and administrative weaknesses. Key forms of this disconnect include:

(a) *Accountability gap due to lack of traceability.* Central governments at times allocate funds to subnational entities without a clear and automated mechanism to track their ultimate use.
(b) *Structural vs. operational gaps.* Systems may appear integrated on paper but function as separate silos in practice. This leads to a disconnect between high-level strategic planning and day-to-day budget execution, with public investment decisions often lacking rigorous appraisal.
(c) *Fragmented mandates.* A lack of coordination and overlapping responsibilities among different ministries creates significant inefficiencies which result in procedural delays and undermine coherent policy implementation.

Digital systems have been consistently identified as a powerful tool to bridge these gaps, although there are challenges and opportunities here as well. For example, the absence of dedicated PFM system modules for local governments in Bangladesh prevents automated data collection and monitoring, forcing reliance on manual reporting and creating information asymmetries between central and local tiers. On the other hand, Viet Nam is deploying software to govern public investments, enabling the central government to better oversee local government projects and improve connectivity between planning and budgeting.

Beyond digitalization, structural reforms are essential for creating durable alignment. Viet Nam, again, provides an insightful case, having merged the two separate ministries responsible for the project pipeline and the budget. This reform was designed to improve horizontal efficiency at the central level by consolidating decision-making. However, a significant vertical challenge remains: the planning process is still relatively top-down, with central government budget parameters guiding local planning exercises and offering limited opportunity for active participation from SNGs. Successfully aligning plans with available funds is only half the battle; the more fundamental challenge lies in generating sufficient resources to fund those plans in the first place.

Enhancing local resource mobilization and fiscal autonomy. Strengthening the ability of SNGs to generate their own-source revenue is fundamental to fostering genuine fiscal autonomy and improving local accountability. Heavy reliance on central transfers can undermine local initiative and create uncertainty in financial planning. There are several significant barriers to local resource mobilization:

(a) *Lack of political will.* Often, local government authorities are not interested in imposing taxes due to electoral concerns. The voting system creates a disincentive, as officials fear that raising taxes will make them unpopular with constituents and jeopardize their re-election prospects.

(b) *Limited fiscal autonomy.* Some SNGs have little to no legal authority to generate revenue. In Fiji, for example, local governments have effectively no fiscal autonomy and cannot collect taxes. Consequently, they must rely on the central government for all project funding, severely limiting their ability to respond to local needs independently.

(c) *Weak administration and enforcement.* Even where the authority to tax exists, administrative weaknesses can hinder revenue collection. In many DMCs there is limited local revenue generation due to weak tax administration and enforcement, a challenge particularly acute in the area of property taxation.

(d) *Unpredictable central transfers.* Over-reliance on central government transfers introduces significant instability into local financial planning. In specific regions in the Kyrgyz Republic, local governments are heavily dependent on transfers from mining revenues, which are seen as both unpredictable and poorly documented, making multi-year investment planning exceptionally difficult.

Despite these barriers, there are good practices and innovative approaches for enhancing own-source revenue by SNGs. For example, by making all procurement projects transparent and publicizing them online, local governments can generate savings, which can then be reinvested into public services. Expanding revenue streams (as evident in Fiji) is another good practice discussed.[34] Further, in Viet Nam an incentive mechanism (innovative on-lending, referred to as *outlanding*) encourages local resource generation. The percentage of central government funds, such as concessional loans, that are on-lent to a local government, is directly tied to the government's performance in raising its own-source revenue. This creates a direct financial incentive for local authorities to be more proactive in mobilizing their own resources.

[34] Local governments in Fiji generated a list of potential new revenue sources, including improving and mandating the collection of city rates, streamlining business licensing processes, introducing user fees for services like parks and rubbish collection, and actively promoting public-private partnerships (PPPs) to fund local infrastructure.

Addressing intractable capacity constraints at local level. Across nearly all countries, capacity constraints at the subnational level can be characterized as being a primary and persistent impediment to development effectiveness. Even with well-aligned plans and adequate funding, a lack of skilled personnel and institutional knowledge can derail implementation and undermine good governance. Some main capacity challenges can be said to be remarkably consistent across all country contexts:

(a) *Human capital flight.* A "brain drain" from local governments to the center is a widespread phenomenon. In many countries, such as Fiji, the situation is even more acute where trained personnel not only move to the capital but often leave the country entirely, resulting in a deep loss of expertise.
(b) *Technical and soft skill gaps.* Local government staff frequently lack adequate training in core competencies. For example, in Bangladesh, it has been recognized that significant capacity building is required to enable local officials to operate the new digital PFM system modules effectively.
(c) *Loss of institutional memory.* High staff rotation means that institutional knowledge is difficult to retain. When trained and experienced individuals leave, their expertise is lost, forcing a continuous and costly cycle of retraining. Digital systems have been mentioned as a potential solution to mitigate this by embedding processes and historical data within the institution itself.

Primacy of political economy. Again and again, any discussion of technical PFM challenges, including at the subnational level, can be traced back to underlying political factors. Issues such as the central government's desire to maintain control over lower tiers of government, the influence of election cycles on local tax policy, and fragmentation among political parties at national and subnational levels have often been seen as the root cause of the technical and administrative problems observed. This underscores the reality that sustainable reform requires a keen awareness of the political context in which it is being implemented.

Transparency as a foundational enabler of strong local governance. Indeed, transparency in the political and economic spheres is not merely a desirable feature but a core mechanism for driving reforms. Examples abound in countries such as Mongolia and the Philippines where the public accessibility of information helps to empower citizens and foster accountability. This improves trust, which, in turn, creates a more favorable environment for resource mobilization and good governance, thus showing that transparency is a foundational enabler of a healthy PFM ecosystem.

Opportunities in digitalization with caveats. Digitalization is seen in a favorable light with respect to effectively addressing the issues mentioned above. But the use of digital tools is not a simple fix. Their success depends on critical prerequisites, including significant investment in capacity building to ensure local staff can use the systems (as seen in Bangladesh, for example), a focus on seamless integration between different government platforms to avoid creating new digital silos (as evident in Mongolia), and the absolute necessity of reliable, regularly updated data to ensure that the information these systems provide is valuable for decision-making.

Importance of understanding local context. Finally, the importance of awareness of the local context in strengthening subnational governance cannot be over-emphasized. Unique geographical and demographic contexts of countries, for example, directly impact the costs of infrastructure, the challenges of service delivery, and the feasibility of certain revenue models. This insight highlights the conclusion that one-size-fits-all approaches to PFM reform and capacity building are unlikely to succeed whether at the central or the subnational level.

Enhancing Domestic Resource Mobilization

Introduction

It has long been accepted that the attainment of the SDGs, as well as any nationally determined vision, such as Mongolia's Vision 2050 (or even ambitious sector-based development goals),[35] will require a substantial amount of resources on a continuing basis. Countries across Asia and the Pacific (and indeed elsewhere in the world) also recognize that there are realistic limits to the levels of foreign direct investment and official development assistance that can flow to their respective economies.[36] Further, as countries such as Bangladesh graduate from the ranks of least-developed countries, their respective governments face the important task of ensuring that their fiscal policies adapt to the changing economic landscape. The loss of trade preferences and concessional financing will necessitate greater reliance on domestic revenue generation and strategic expenditure planning.

Analysis done by the Millennium Corporate Challenge has shown that, at $5.5 trillion annually, domestic resources make up the largest source of total resources available to developing countries (**Figure 5**).

Figure 5. Sources of Investments for Development

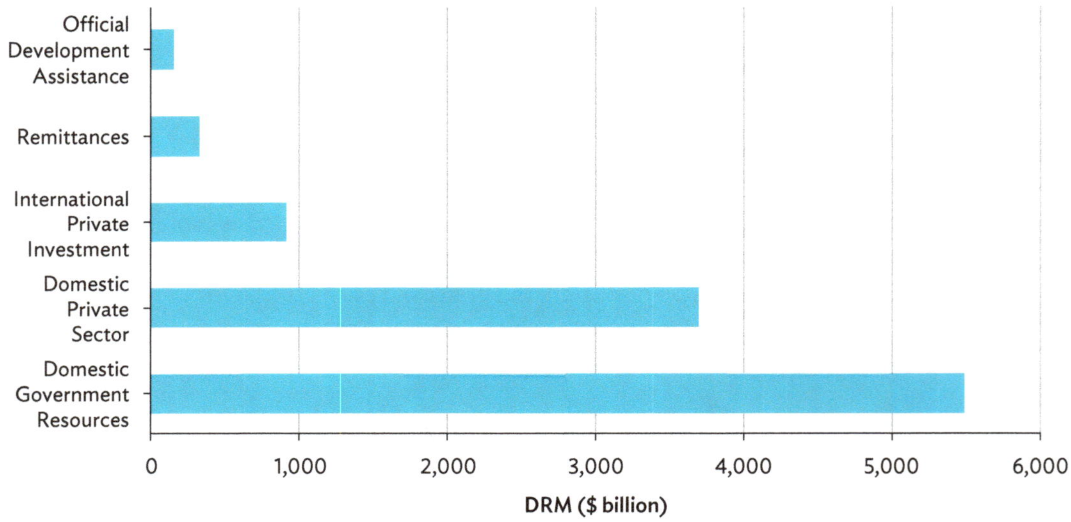

DRM = domestic resource mobilization.

Source: European Report on Development and World Bank (*not dated*). https://www.mcc.gov/initiatives/initiative/domestic-resource-mobilization/ (accessed 18 August 2025).

Given this scenario, the focus on the need to enhance DRM in countries is logical. The Addis Tax Initiative in 2015 declared that DRM is at the core of ensuring achievement of the SDGs. This resource enhancement can be a result of various policy actions, including revenue enhancement from taxes, a product of fiscal consolidation, or other means.

[35] Such as the Philippines' focus on a "Build-Build-Build" drive on infrastructure development that demanded a total of about $20 billion a year in sustained investments from 2016 to 2022. This translated to a public infrastructure spending rise from 4.5% of gross domestic product in 2016 to 7.3% by 2022 (see ADB. 2018b. *Asian Development Outlook 2018: How Technology Affects Jobs*. p. 275).

[36] For example, foreign direct investment inflows to Bangladesh have historically been low relative to other economies in the region (during 2013–2023, inflows as a percentage of GDP stood at 0.8%, while it was 4.6% in Viet Nam) (see ADB. 2025b. *Asian Development Outlook: Trade Uncertainty Challenges – Resilience in Asia and the Pacific*. p.145). As for ODA flows, only a handful of developed countries have consistently upheld the binding commitment to spend 0.7% of their national budget on development aid.

Tax Policy and Administration

In the domain of public resources, those from taxes are the most appealing. Proposals to strengthen tax systems and mobilize domestic resources seek to cover several areas, such as: (a) enhancing the capacity of the government to raise tax collection; (b) broadening the domestic tax base; (c) putting in place the right tax policies (i.e., those that are fair and effective); (d) improving domestic tax compliance; (e) stemming cross-border and domestic tax evasion; and (f) enhancing cooperation among national authorities and international organizations.

The enhancement of tax collection is the first port of call to mobilize greater resources, especially since tax-to-gross domestic product (GDP) ratios in DMCs are still on average below 20% compared to almost double the amount in OECD countries. Widening the tax net has been an important measure that governments have been pursuing to generate more domestic resources. They are also increasingly using digital technology to enhance tax collections, largely by streamlining tax administration but also by bringing in previous non-filers into the tax net. The treatment of taxes generally focuses on both the policy and its administration. **Box 4** shows the successful experiences of Maldives in this regard.

Box 4. Revenue Mobilization in Maldives

Maldives achieved historically high levels of revenue collection in the form of taxes through aggressive tax administration reforms, which led to a rise in tax-to-gross domestic product ratio from 9.8% in 2010 to 28.0% in 2016 (an increase of almost 300% in only 6 years). However, the ratio stood at 23.5% in 2023 (given some economic difficulties in the immediate preceding years). Some key lessons were documented from the performance of Maldives Inland Revenue Authority (MIRA):

1. On tax policy, the strong political commitment from government helped spur the reform process.
2. MIRA's independence was legislated, and the law contained unambiguous provisions on tax collection.
3. On tax administration, there was considerable focus on: (a) use of external expertise (which enabled MIRA to push through measures which benefitted from external successes); and (b) a strong training regime (which was also differentiated by target groups so that bespoke capacity enhancement measures could be put in place).

Source: ADB. 2017. *Fast-Track Tax Reform: Lessons from Maldives.*

Tax policy measures in DMCs have generally tended to be rather piecemeal and entailing high administrative costs. They have sought to: (a) entice the private sector to play a greater role in the economy so that public sector commitments to development expenditures are channeled to social goals (where private sector investments are not readily targeted); (b) ensure adequate transparency of tax exemptions and assessment of the impact of such exemptions on fiscal management; (c) take into consideration the welfare of SNGs of the tax policy; and (d) appropriately target tax incentives in that there should be clarity on how much these cost in terms of foregone revenue and on their overall impact.

On **tax administration**, tax enforcement is a challenge in all DMCs, as it is generally a struggle to get taxpayers to pay taxes for a variety of reasons, including that the system is rather complex, or the relevant government entity has inadequate institutional capacity to ensure that taxes are indeed being paid. The challenge is aggravated by the fact that there is generally a fairly large unregistered informal economy. DMCs have sought to address these challenges through various means, including stronger focus on large taxpayers (e.g., in the Kyrgyz Republic), rationalizing and reforming organizational structure and business processes (such as in Bangladesh, which has carried out customs tariff restructuring and rationalization in the recent past), or risk-based audit management (as seen in several DMCs).

Some of the generic weaknesses highlighted on tax administration across DMCs are reflected in some issues that Bangladesh is facing on this matter. Reconciliation is not immediately done for tax assessments and arrears; and revenue data collection accounting is done on a cash basis, with no arrears recorded in the Integrated Budget and Accounting System (iBAS++). This creates a gap in vital revenue information, thus impacting a substantial loss of resources for the budget. Furthermore, due to the fragmentation of tax administration, the tax system is characterized by high degrees of informality, a fair amount of discretion, and the regular negotiation of tax liabilities.

Efforts to enhance tax revenues by DMCs across the region are exemplified in **Box 5**.

Box 5. Efforts by Developing Member Countries to Enhance Tax Revenues

Fiji[a]

Several reforms have been put in place by the Fiji Revenue and Customs Service. These include:

- The move toward a single broad-based value-added tax (VAT) rate to streamline lodgments of returns.
- The establishment of new tax audit units for large taxpayers.
- The creation of a support center for small and medium-sized enterprises.
- Launch of a new compliance improvement strategy to encourage voluntary compliance.
- Rollout of the new tax information system in 2023, which facilitates online tax filing.

Kyrgyz Republic[b]

- To simplify fiscal procedures, reduce tax burden, formalize "grey" businesses, and form a fair tax system, the government is pursuing the implementation of tax reforms aimed at digitalizing tax and customs administration. Full integration of tax and customs information systems is also sought.
- The government is committed to joining the Global Forum on Transparency and Exchange of Information for Tax Purposes and the Organisation for Economic Co-operation and Development/Group of Twenty Inclusive Framework on Base Erosion and Profit Shifting.

Philippines[c]

- Broaden income and VAT bases and automate tax and customs administration.
- Government's MTFF 2022–2028 contains a fiscal consolidation plan that calls for DRM measures that target increased revenues to support post-COVID-19 pandemic fiscal sustainability.
- Government's reform targets in this area now include DRM policies and legal frameworks enhanced so as to mobilize additional tax revenues of $4.5 billion (1.3% of gross domestic product) annually. It has also created legal frameworks for national and local taxation policies.

Sources: ADB's Pacific Economic Monitor, December 2023; ADB's Policy-Based Loan for Subprogram 1 on sustainable fiscal management and governance improvement program (project number: 57193-001) (June 2024); ADB's Policy-Based Loan for Subprogram 1 on DRM (project number: 56288-001), October 2023.

How Else to Mobilize More?

Governments all over the world have faced this question; evidence from across the spectrum of countries shows that several measures have been considered to mobilize more resources, some more successfully than others (**Figure 6**).

Figure 6. Resource Mobilization Scope Beyond Taxes

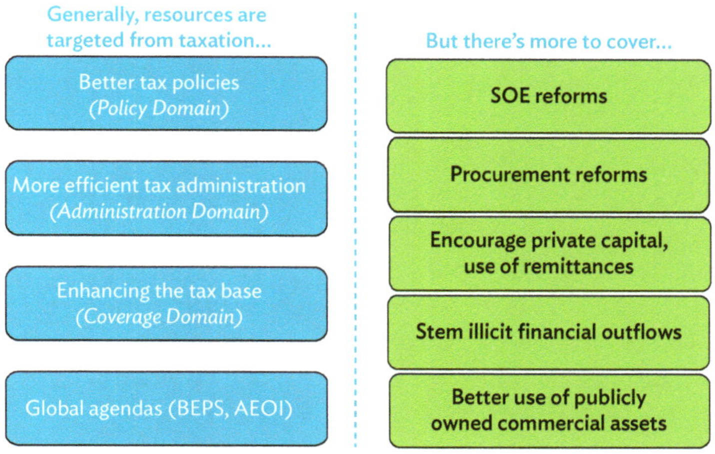

AEOI = Automatic Exchange of Information, BEPS = base erosion and profit shifting, EU = European Union, FATF = Financial Action Task Force, GDP = gross domestic product, SOE = state-owned enterprise.

Source: Authors.

Increasingly, governments are also capitalizing on the availability of digital technologies to improve tax compliance and enforcement such that their revenues may increase as a result of better coverage and capture. Such technologies not only help broaden the tax base (by netting new taxpayers, for example) but also enable governments to identify the true levels of taxes they are owed – all of this at lower costs and with less interaction with tax officials (thus avoiding risks of bribes). It is thus easy to see why digitalization is being seen as the preferred method to minimize tax avoidance. It is also worth noting that, along with public procurement, taxation tends to be considered as a high-impact service and prioritized in national digital integration efforts.

Minimizing tax avoidance. In 2017, OECD estimated that $240 billion/year of corporate income tax revenue is lost as a result of base erosion and profit shifting (BEPS).[37] In the Philippines alone, revenue losses from international tax avoidance were estimated at $7.4 billion annually, equivalent to 2.7% of GDP.[38] Global efforts have now been ramped up as evident in initiatives such as anti-money laundering and combating the financing of terrorism, and stolen asset recovery.

Instituting procurement reforms. Evaluations of public procurement processes show procurement losses that could be reversed and thus provide extra resources to governments. Efficiencies in the public procurement regime are increasingly saving monies through streamlined bidding processes (such as through e-Procurement) and efficient contract management systems. This is evident, for example, in Mongolia where ADB's recent support for strengthening the government's e-procurement platform and enhancing capacities in selected agencies has

[37] BEPS refers to actions taken by multinational companies to avoid paying taxes in one jurisdiction by nominally moving their profits to a jurisdiction where the incidence of tax is lower or where tax breaks and exemptions mean much lower taxes need to be paid.

[38] A. Cobham, P. Jansky. 2017. Global Distribution of Revenue Loss from Tax Avoidance: Re-Estimation and Country Results. *WIDER Working Paper* 2017/55. World Institute for Development Economics Research.

yielded substantive benefits.[39] Further, in its 2021 Public Expenditure Review assessment for Nepal, the World Bank asserted that about 60% of Nepal's annual government budget is implemented through procurement, with the procurement of goods and services accounting for 43% of total spending in FY2021 at the provincial and local level.[40] These numbers reflect the importance of public procurement reforms in strengthening PFM and achieving overall development effectiveness, especially when one considers that some of the largest control gaps exist in this space.

Stemming illicit fund outflows. There are considerable amounts of resources at stake in illicit fund outflows.[41] In January 2019, Global Financial Integrity estimated that illicit flows to and from developing countries were worth more than a fifth of their total trade with developed countries.[42] The Stolen Asset Recovery Initiative of the World Bank and the United Nations estimates that $20–40 billion a year is stolen from developing countries. ADB country diagnostic work shows that illicit financial outflows from Bangladesh alone between 2009 and 2023 was in the range of about $234 billion, at an average annual outflow of about $16 billion (equivalent to 3.4% of its GDP for 2024). It has been estimated that, if taxed (at 25%), the illicit outflows from Bangladesh would have generated revenues equivalent to about 9.8% of total tax earnings. These are very sobering numbers indeed.

There is now international pressure, led by the Group of 20 countries, to crack down on illicit financial flows (tax evasion, cross-border corruption, money laundering, terrorism financing, etc.). Still, many developing countries continue to lack the necessary legislative and regulatory infrastructure to be fully compliant with global standards and requirements.

Strengthening public investment management. Another method of raising more domestic resources is through public investment management reforms, because these will increase efficiencies that will invariably yield greater returns on investments. The IMF argues that, on average, inefficiencies exist in around 40% of public investment processes, and that the economic dividends from closing this gap are substantial.[43]

The IMF also argues that strengthening 15 key institutions that shape the planning, allocation, and implementation of public investments could close up to two-thirds of the public investment efficiency gap. This frees up a substantial amount of potential investment resources. Nevertheless, for reforms to be effective, governments need to target different measures based on their level of development. For instance, for emerging economies, the focus should be on instituting greater rigor and transparency on the selection and approval of investment projects. On the other hand, for low-income countries, fund management and the monitoring of project investments should be prioritized.

More prudent fiscal policy. There is also evidence of greater resource mobilization through the practice of a more prudent fiscal policy, anchored on a robust legal framework. For example, the Government of Timor-Leste has in the past pursued a fiscal policy based on using oil revenues to front-load infrastructure and human capital

[39] See ADB. 2022a. *TA Completion Report for TA 9158 (Mongolia: Strengthening of Public Procurement for Improved Project Implementation).* This demonstrates that public procurement properly carried out yields substantial dividends. This data point is a bit dated, but it makes a strong case – in Nepal, the "nation-wide savings from e-GP system could reach up to 20% of procurement costs (estimated at $14.8 billion in Fiscal Year 2010)" (Program completion report of Nepal Strengthening Public Management Program (#36172-063), Asian Development Bank, November 2017, p. 14). Even in advanced countries, public procurement reforms have yielded substantial dividends (a study done by RAND Europe for the European Union in 2016 showed that public procurement corruption in the EU was worth €5 billion). By implementing a union-wide e-procurement system, it could bring down the cost of corruption by an estimated €920 million; R. Collins. 2016. Corruption Costs EU 'up to 900 billion Euros a year' (accessed 17 August 2025).

[40] NRs1.474 trillion was the government's national budget in FY2021/22, 60% of which yields approximately NRs885 billion. Assuming a minimum of 20% reduction in procurement costs through reforms (the lower limit of what ADB, OECD, World Bank, IMF, and others have argued; (see, e.g., IMF, 2023), this amounts to greater than NRs176 billion (or $1.3 billion) in nominal savings a year.

[41] See, for example, Kar and Freitas. 2012.

[42] *The Economist*. 2019. Dirty Money: Leaky Borders. 2 February. p. 62.

[43] IMF. 2015. *Making Public Investment More Efficient.*

investments to pursue ambitious development goals. The country's Estimated Sustainable Income has gradually declined over time due to the erosion of petroleum wealth which, combined with weak DRM, has necessitated financing the annual deficit mainly by excess withdrawals from the Petroleum Fund, and to a lesser extent by cash balances and external loans. In the absence of a clear fiscal policy expressed in law, the practice of using excess withdrawals threatens the sustainability of the Petroleum Fund and may lead to high implicit costs in the form of foregone future revenues (considering the quality of public spending).

One subset of prudent fiscal policy is infrastructure governance, which is central to how public funds can be sustainably managed. It is estimated that more than 50% of infrastructural investments go to waste in low-income countries.[44] Resolving such weaknesses would not only reduce the costs of the investments (thus positively impacting the fiscal situation of the country) but also minimize operations and maintenance costs on public assets by freeing up more resources for development expenditures. Good infrastructure governance implies, at the front-end, rigorous processes of project costing, selection, and appraisal just as effective execution is also critical else the impact on the economy is not likely to be substantial or sustainable.

Focusing on robust public–private partnerships. Related to the point made above on enhanced public investment management is that of public–private partnership (PPP). Increasing reliance on PPP also ensures that governments generate revenues through savings on investments that will be provided by the private sector. Effective PPPs, however, require that the public sector has adequate absorptive capacity, not something that is readily evident in all DMCs. Also, the scale of PPP funds needed is substantial: in 2017, ADB estimated that, to fill the remaining gaps in infrastructure investments alone in developing Asia (for 2016–2020), the private sector would have to increase investments from about $63 billion to as high as $250 billion a year.[45] These levels of financing needs have surely increased substantially since then.

Enlightened asset use and management. An appealing measure that governments may consider is the better use of vastly available assets such as land and government-owned commercial assets (e.g., by SOEs).[46] This is considered to be one of the most underrated resource-saving measures in low-income countries. When governments have to tighten their belts, asset maintenance tends to become the first victim. This, in the long run, reduces the value of public assets, because maintenance gaps lead to faster depreciation. This is why it is argued that if public assets were managed better, government coffers would enjoy a boost.[47] For this, governments will need to provide adequate recurring budgets for maintenance of assets.

Asset management is also related to infrastructure maintenance, which hardly appears to be a top priority of many developing countries (encapsulated in the "build-neglect-rebuild" paradigm).[48] Several measures to maintain assets can be identified, including: (a) direct earmarking for asset maintenance in the budget; (b) providing incentives and service targets for specific asset classes, which will give impetus for ensuring the sustenance of the infrastructural asset; (c) strengthening asset management through risk-based maintenance approaches; and (d) using long-term maintenance contracts based on formal estimates of maintenance requirements taking into account the risk assessment carried out in (c).

44 G. Schwartz, et al. (eds). 2020. How Strong Infrastructure Governance Can End Waste in Public Investment. September 3. See also their book (with the same title) that this blog refers to.

45 ADB. 2017a. *Asian Development Outlook 2017: Transcending the Middle-Income Challenge.*

46 In 2018, it was reported that at the central government level these have a book value of $75 trillion, and about the same at the local government level (C. Giles. 2018. IMF Urges Governments to Focus on State Assets. *Financial Times*. 10 October).

47 *The Economist*. 2018. Public Wealth: How to Spend It. 20 October. pp. 67–68.

48 Pacific Region Infrastructure Facility. 2013. *Infrastructure Maintenance in the Pacific: Challenging the Build-Neglect-Rebuild Paradigm.*

Maximizing use of remittances. Another measure to target greater DRM is encouraging private capital largely through use of remittances (estimated by the World Bank to be around $818 billion in 2023, up from $600 billion in 2016). Nepal, the Kyrgyz Republic, and many other countries rely on remittances as a major foreign-currency source of income (indeed, both were in the range of low 30% as a share of GDP in 2024).

Yet not much of this is invested in any formal manner (the funds themselves often tend to be transferred through non-official channels). Opening new investment channels should enable some of these funds to be brought in through formal means. One specific measure that has been discussed to maximize government revenues from the remittance process is to apply the distributed ledger technology-based clearing and settlement process.

Efficiency of revenue mobilization. Few governments can hope to take purposive action to attain their development objectives without focusing on both constraining expenditures and expanding revenues. To enhance the efficiency of revenue mobilization, governments can target informed tax policies and effective tax administration measures. Use of appropriate technologies, reliance on risk-based audit management, streamlined tax appeals systems, and other such whole-of-government measures have proven to be effective in enhancing the efficiency of revenue mobilization in DMCs.

Some Key Issues to Note in Domestic Resource Mobilization

As governments begin to look into additional sources of domestic revenues, more issues will certainly emerge that will require their attention. ***Greater DRM at local level*** is, as yet, an underemphasized option, because most measures have focused on the central government. Although some work has been done in this space, more consideration should be given to enhancing the ability of local governments to generate their own revenues. Improved resource mobilization at the local level through fiscal consolidation and efficient intergovernmental fiscal transfers should be complemented by local revenue enhancement measures. This would have the added advantage of strengthening the fiscal position of SNGs.

Focusing on greater engagement with allies such as Office of Auditor General and Public Accounts Committee. Credible and well-regarded bodies such as these two, whose mandate it is to scrutinize resource use in the public sector and report any mismanagement as well as direct actions to be taken, will help to enhance accountability in the public sector. Effective actions taken on their recommendations will yield substantial revenue streams to DMCs in the form of stemming losses in the system as well as recouping monies owed from individuals and firms for unpaid, but due, taxes.

It is also critical for governments to ***find the right balance*** between tax policy and tax administration (both are equally important in the drive to raise more domestic resources). There is a tendency to center attention on tax administration given that it directly impacts the level and scale of tax revenues, and the results can be very visible. But a large part of the specific impact determination is how the nature of tax administration is conditioned by the underlying policy.

Practical measures. Country experiences on the subject of DRM showcase several practical measures that can be considered for adoption; these include:

(a) **Citizen-centric incentives and data integration are proven, high-impact administrative reforms that build public trust.** Strategies like Mongolia's VAT refund mobile application, which empowers citizens to co-enforce compliance, and Fiji's mandatory linkage of tax numbers to digital payment apps demonstrate how technology can be used to foster a partnership between the state and taxpayers.

(b) **Systematic, data-driven frameworks for SOE oversight offer a politically pragmatic path to reducing fiscal drain.** The Philippines' use of a performance scorecard to abolish or merge non-performing SOEs and, further afield, New Zealand's partial ownership model that improves dividends without ceding full control, provide replicable models for rationalizing state assets.

(c) **Reform efforts will fail without directly confronting political economy constraints; these are the root cause of DRM underperformance.** It is important to note that technical solutions are insufficient when faced with challenges such as policy capture, which can create a systemic preference for foreign aid over domestic mobilization due to rent-seeking opportunities, and deep public trust deficits.

Social contract. The most sustainable gains in compliance and administration often come from measures that strengthen the underlying social contract between the state and its citizens. A core challenge in many countries is fostering a greater willingness to pay taxes. The experience from Bangladesh highlights the power of direct public engagement and advocacy. The National Board of Revenue has moved to address this by holding public awareness meetings to communicate a clear message: domestic resources are essential for national development. This strategy aims to build a sense of shared responsibility, shifting the public perception of taxation from a mere obligation to a civic contribution. By making the link between taxes paid and development outcomes explicit, such campaigns can begin to build the public trust necessary for an improved tax system.

Simplifying systems and empowering taxpayers. Complexity is the enemy of compliance, and DMCs are taking steps to address this. Fiji's reforms, for example, in simplifying the tax structure have made it more transparent and easier to navigate for citizens and businesses. Beyond policy simplification, governments should also empower taxpayers directly by providing training and awareness programs. These initiatives help citizens and businesses file their own tax returns, reducing their reliance on, and the associated costs of, middlemen. By demystifying the filing process, the government not only lowers compliance costs for taxpayers but also encourages more direct and accurate reporting.

Creating citizen-centric incentives. Not necessarily suitably emphasized in the discussions on DRM and tax systems are citizen-centric incentives. Mongolia, for example, demonstrates the success of creating a powerful, citizen-driven compliance mechanism through its VAT refund system, managed via the "eBarent" mobile application. The system works by allowing citizens to scan their purchase receipts and receive a 2% VAT refund directly. This simple incentive has created a strong partnership between the government and citizens by turning consumers into active participants in ensuring tax compliance. Citizens are now highly motivated to demand official receipts for all purchases, effectively creating a nationwide, crowd-sourced audit function that discourages businesses from under-reporting sales. The impact has been significant, with VAT revenue growing to account for approximately 20% of total tax revenues by 2024. The government plans to strengthen this incentive further by increasing the refund rate to 5% for larger purchases, signaling its commitment to this successful model.

The foundational role of data integration. The ability to integrate and share data across government agencies is a critical, yet often challenging, component of modern tax administration. In many countries, a significant obstacle to effective tax administration is the existence of data silos between the tax authority, customs, and banking authorities. This segregation makes cross-checking information to verify income or transactions almost impossible, creating opportunities for evasion and limiting the effectiveness of enforcement. Linking the national tax identification number to digital payment applications (as done in Fiji, for example) offers a way out of this adverse situation. This integration allows the tax authorities to track transactions effectively, significantly increasing revenue collection from the growing sphere of online business activities. This comparison underscores that technological tools are only as effective as the regulatory and institutional frameworks that enable data sharing.[49]

[49] DMCs in Asia and the Pacific could learn valuable lessons from the experiences of Estonia, long considered a trailblazer in digital and information systems for public policy and service delivery purposes. Its X-Road interoperability platform greatly facilitates real-time data exchange among agencies, thus directly contributing to effective, efficient, and equitable service delivery. In Estonia, as elsewhere, public organizations have their own information systems to process information relevant to their own clients, beneficiaries, and stakeholders. What X-Road does is serve as a distributed information exchange platform enabling different systems to communicate across government agencies in real time. Data security is highly emphasized in X-Road, and the platform is structured to be interoperable and technically easy for all members of the system that use it; GovTech Intelligence Hub. 2025. *Smarter Data Exchange: How X-Road Became a Model for Digital Public Infrastructure* (accessed 2 January 2026).

The politics of policy. While administrative improvements are essential, the most significant potential for increasing revenue lies in tax policy reform. However, this is also the most politically challenging component of DRM, often confronting deeply entrenched interests and public resistance. There are generally two binding political economy challenges that consistently undermine tax reform efforts: (a) policy and institutional capture, whereby collusion between politics and business is often cited as a major driver of tax evasion and weak enforcement;[50] and (b) public trust deficit, whereby a widespread public perception of corruption erodes confidence in how tax revenues are used and creates strong political opposition to any new taxes or rate increases, as citizens are unwilling to contribute more to a system they believe is wasteful or corrupt.

By extension, then, ***political commitment*** to fundamental reforms in DRM enhancement is an absolute must. The need for governments to demonstrate and sustain strong political commitment to DRM, particularly on those steps that have been recommended, will necessitate them to make tough calls, such as on (a) strong tax-related reforms; (b) suitably addressing the overall and system-wide problem of mismanagement and of corruption in the public sector; and (c) sustaining reforms in public financial and public expenditure systems, including public investment management. It is this final topic on PFM reforms that is discussed next.

Improving Public Financial and Public Expenditure Systems

Challenges in strengthening public financial and public expenditure systems are evident across multiple aspects of PFM in various countries. Because these issues closely align with the components of country systems (as discussed earlier), this study largely draws its analysis from those elements.

Budgeting

On **budget classification**, the intent is to ensure the robustness of the budgeting function by **aligning it to global standards**, especially with respect to: (a) consistency of budget information and (b) enabling expenditure tracking through the budget cycle. While the consistency of budget information is considered acceptable in many countries (with the PEFA scores generally being higher on this indicator), there remain issues with expenditure tracking. Such issues generally pertain to the adequacy of the needed evidence base.

Instances of misalignment can also result if some of the basic foundations of program-based budgeting have been put in place, such as a 3-year MTEF, but budget submissions are still prepared according to the traditional line-item format. In other words, while the Ministry of Finance (MOF) may prepare a 3-year MTEF with expenditure ceilings for each spending agency, if the program budgeting classification of the budget for the country is on a parallel system, then that has little real impact on the planning or implementation of the budget.

When budgeting is carried out properly, it is expected that the **budget preparation** process will be orderly and timely (as evident in many DMCs in the study region), and that it provides adequate information to support robust assumptions and budget proposals. The focus on assumptions is important, because budget levels are entirely dependent upon them, and transparency is greatly enhanced when the government makes public the underlying assumptions on the exchange and interest rates supporting the budget, as well as the modeled scenarios.

50 This dynamic, described as "policy capture," not only facilitates tax evasion by powerful interests but also creates a systemic preference within government for foreign aid over domestic mobilization, as external financing can present greater opportunities for rent-seeking.

This is evident in Bangladesh where efforts are ongoing to include risks in macroeconomic forecasts regarding revenues and expenditures. While the situation in Nepal is slightly more complex given that the federal and SNGs have different schedules and provisions for budget preparation, the Philippines has consistently submitted its proposed budget to the House of Representatives usually a day after the President delivers the State of the Nation Address, allowing Congress sufficient time to review and scrutinize it.

Issues in budgeting and budget preparation in Viet Nam may possibly set to be more complex given that fundamental politico-bureaucratic-administrative changes are underway. The primary change is the amalgamation and repositioning of the current local governance system with one that is more streamlined with considerably fewer local bodies (from 63 provinces and cities to 34 such entities as of July 2025). If there are gaps in institutional capacity at the subnational level, there are likely to be consequent impact on the strength of budgeting at that level, such as in operationalizing the PFM requirements.

One particular issue in budgeting is that of **transparency**,[51] the lack of which leads to, among others, manipulation of national accounts data related to GDP growth, private investment, inflation, and other economic indicators.[52] Related to budget transparency is the timely availability of budget documents, financial reports, or information on debt obligations, public expenditures, etc. for public access, which has been observed as being limited in many DMCs. A further issue is on the linkage between medium-term planning and budgeting. In several DMCs (for example, Bangladesh, Fiji, Pakistan, and Palau) there is a general lack of costed strategies in some sectors, which weakens the integration between national development plans and budget frameworks.

A key feature of the PFM system in some countries is that the budgetary framework does not include SOEs and extra-budgetary funds,[53] hence, key spending decisions are not always guided by macro considerations or made within the overall fiscal framework. This gives the governments more scope in deciding about payments and subsidies as it is subject to less pressure to be accountable to taxpayers through elected institutions. This has consequential adverse impact on the preparation of realistic budgets as the allocated budgets for specific projects will not correspond to the actual payments made throughout the fiscal year.

Treasury

The primary focus in **budget control** is on whether there are adequate systems and procedures for such control (for example, evidenced by high expenditure outturn and minimal variations in expenditure composition). Underspending in some sectors is explained by procurement bottlenecks, land acquisition issues, and slow project implementation.

Improper spending under annual development programs is also an issue across many DMCs where often less than half of the funds are spent in the first 9 months and the rest is spent hurriedly in the last quarter—a clear indicator of weak budget controls. Even in Bhutan, deemed a frontier DMC for purposes of this study, it was observed that agencies tend to spend more towards the last quarter. For example, the Royal Audit Authority has noted that procuring entities do not plan their purchases and that most of the capital expenditure is carried out towards the

51 The issue of transparency in budgeting is at the center of the discussions on good governance when it comes to fiscal policy and arrangements. After all, resource allocation for budget priorities reflects government's public policy focus and if transparency in this process is not evident then public trust in government's action is diminished.

52 For example, the interim government in Bangladesh has made strong efforts to correct the system to collect national data on exports pursuant to the difference in evidence that was put out by the central bank and the Export Promotion Board (to the tune of nearly $14 billion mismatch in export data in July–April of fiscal year 2024). The government's White Paper on the Economy identified this "deceptive data"; R. Mirdha, and Md. Zaman. 2024. Bangladesh Moves to Put Export Data System in Order: Real-time Data Platform Will Be Rolled Out (accessed 13 January 2026). See also Center for Policy Dialogue, 2024. *White Paper 2024 – State of the Bangladesh Economy: Dissection of a Development Narrative*. Dhaka.

53 United Nations Conference on Trade and Development. 2021. *The Least Developed Countries Report 2020: Productive Capacities for the New Decade*. p. 107.

last quarter of the financial year.[54] Moreover, since procuring entities are generally inclined to spend their remaining budget rather than relinquish it, they tend to conduct unplanned procurements when they anticipate surplus funds from different budgetary allocations.

The **Treasury Single Account** (TSA) is a set of linked accounts that are centralized at a single bank to facilitate the consolidation of bank accounts and through which the government transacts every receipt and payment. There are some DMCs (such as Fiji) that do not have a TSA, and others (such as Kiribati) that have nascent TSA systems. The presence of fragmented banking arrangements and multiple bank accounts held across agencies reduces visibility over government cash resources and limits the efficiency of cash management.

Other nuances are seen in the Kyrgyz Republic which has an effective TSA but externally financed investment transactions take place through commercial banks in accordance with the terms agreed with each funding agency. In Bangladesh, SOEs operate separate accounts in both state-owned and commercial banks but the government is taking steps to expand TSA coverage and reduce cash held outside its framework.

For effective **cash management and expenditure arrears,** governments in recent years have been increasing efforts to adopt electronic fund transfers and automation of transactions. This means the nature and scope of cash management will necessarily be impacted. On the subject of expenditure arrears, the focus is on whether the DMC has a low stock of expenditure payment arrears, and just as important, whether there is a centralized and regular monitoring of such arrears (as in Mongolia). This requires a robust financial management information system (FMIS) for accurate recording of invoice dates and goods receipt dates. As good practice in this area, the e-Treasury System in Georgia allows for real-time recording and monitoring of arrears through its module for recording invoices, where it is possible to generate data on the overdue debt of any budgetary unit in real time.

Accounting

Governments are keen to ensure the **integrity of financial information** through constant checks and verification of recording practices, and reconciliation of data from different sources in a timely manner.[55] Here, too, a robust FMIS plays a key role as it helps in commitment control and in timely reconciliation of revenue accounts. Reconciliation of central government bank accounts is commonly mandated to occur monthly in many countries, such as Pakistan and Tonga, while jurisdictions like Azerbaijan and Indonesia perform daily reconciliation of accounts through their respective TSA system.

Also important are internal controls for expenditures and investment project monitoring, and satisfactory compliance with payment rules and procedures, especially when such controls are integrated and implemented through an FMIS. Some examples are (a) daily reconciliation of unexplained or unusual transactions through a smart payment system connected to the central bank's automated clearing house and the government FMIS, which are then cleared by the end of the interim and annual reporting periods (Mongolia); (b) enforcement of segregation of duties through the FMIS (Samoa, Vanuatu, and Palau); and (c) implementation of strict compliance with payment rules and commitment controls through the Treasury FIMS to ensure compliance with budget allocations (Tajikistan). Many DMCs rely on their FMIS for real-time monitoring and data integrity.

54 For example, it was reported that "the utilisation of monthly and quarterly capital expenditure for three consecutive financial years of 2019-20 to 2021–22 revealed a rush of capital expenditure towards the last quarter of the financial year, representing 54.95% compared to previous quarters which represents only 8.99%, 17.00% and 19.05% for first, second and third quarters respectively."; Royal Audit Authority. 2022. Press release. 7 December (accessed 13 January 2026).

55 One particular set of financial information is related to that on government fixed assets, information on which needs to be included in a fixed asset registry. In countries that do not have such a registry, such as Bangladesh (currently being established) this compromises the degree of robust information the government has on asset management. Elsewhere, there is evidence of such provisions at the sectoral level; in Kazakhstan, for example, the National Quality Center for Road Assets is engaged in development of needed sectoral guidelines, revisions of applicable national regulations, and production of manuals and public outreach materials.

Effective accounting also demands robust **internal controls** for expenditures and monitoring of investment projects. For maximum effectiveness, there should also be segregation of duties[56] and expenditure commitment controls, as well as satisfactory compliance with payment rules and procedures. In Mongolia, for example, compliance with the rules for processing and recording transactions is generally high (with most exceptions being properly authorized and justified and a senior staff member in the central Treasury overseeing daily internal control).

Internal auditing functions are important since they ensure that the accounts are properly kept and updated (covering areas such as payroll, procurement, revenue management, capital projects, cash payments, etc.). Relatedly, there is premium placed on efficient follow-up on findings and recommendations. As the focus is on integrity, it is advisable to have a separate unit that is responsible for data integrity, which is not evident across the DMCs covered in this study. Financial data integrity is a key component of the accounting and reporting pillars of a country's PFM system. The PEFA assessment tool pays substantial attention to this, with particular focus on account reconciliation and data integrity issues in suspense and advance accounts.

Strong **internal auditing** processes and systems are also key here, including: (a) that the DMC has an operational internal audit function (either centralized, or in each entity); (b) that it is undertaken with a high coverage level; (c) that it is administratively independent; (d) that professional internal audit standards are applied; (e) that internal audit plans are prepared and implemented; and (f) that there is efficient follow-up on the findings and recommendations. Good practices in internal auditing in Bhutan are highlighted in **Box 6**.

Box 6. Internal Auditing Practices in Bhutan

The internal audit performance in Bhutan's public financial management (PFM) system improved from C+ in the 2016 PEFA to B+ in the 2022 Public Expenditure and Financial Accountability (PEFA). A large part of the improvement in the system is due to the fact that the government has an operational central internal audit function at the Central Coordinating Agency (CCA) under the MOF.

The CCA's core mandate under the Public Finance Act (2012) covers several areas:

- Governance of the internal audit functions;
- Administration of internal audit services;
- Management of internal audit activities; and
- Strengthening of internal control system management.

The government adopts the International Standards for the Professional Practice of Internal Auditing issued by the Institute of Internal Auditors. As per the 2022 PEFA assessment, during the period under review the government had 12 functioning internal audit units in central government agencies and 15 internal audit units in SNG agencies. There are also established internal audit guidelines that include the Charter Internal Audit Manual, Code of Conduct of Internal Auditors, Internal Auditing Standards and Quality Assurance, and Improvement Program Guidelines.

Finally, the annual internal audit plans are formulated before the start of the fiscal year based on risk-based audit plans. There are also mechanisms to follow up on internal audit observations and recommendations, and significant improvement on management response was noted from 40% in fiscal year (FY) 2019 to 92% in FY2022.

Source: *Country diagnostic study for the Bhutan CPS*, 2023.

[56] This segregation of duties works as: (a) expenditure transactions are authorized by the budget holders in spending bodies; (b) recording and accounting are undertaken by the Treasury; (c) the receipt of goods and services are certified by other officials of the ordering body; and (d) audit is undertaken by internal and external audit services that have no operational link with the transactions concerned.

In Georgia and other DMCs, records cannot be created or modified without leaving an audit trail. Audit trails generated from the TSA provide information on who accessed the data, who initiated the transaction, who approved the transaction, the time of day and date of entry, the type of entry, what fields of information it contained, and what files it updated. These bits of information ensure that a rigorous audit is possible which enables accurate information to be made available while carrying out the external audit to follow.

An internal audit function is established in almost all government agencies across the DMCs, although with varying degrees of implementation and coverage. Azerbaijan, Kiribati, and Nepal have a central agency (e.g., the MOF) that performs internal audit functions for the government. On the other hand, DMCs such as Cambodia, Mongolia, and the Philippines have a decentralized internal audit framework in which internal audit functions are established within and performed by each government agency. There are also DMCs such as Nauru and Tuvalu that lack a legislative and institutional framework for internal audit.

All DMCs in the study region seek to prioritize internal audit functions as part of their efforts at PFM reforms. Such reforms may need to focus on addressing some common implementation gaps, even in DMCs with established internal audit functions, such as staffing shortages and capacity constraints, limited scope and operational gaps, and institutional fragmentation and a lack of independence. To this end, the efforts of various DMCs tell a compelling story on the reforms being sought, for example:

(a) *Bangladesh*: the MOF has developed an internal audit charter and a risk-based internal audit manual, aligned with the Institute of Internal Auditors standards.
(b) *Georgia*: established five types of engagements (i.e., financial, compliance, system, performance, and ICT audits) and implemented internal audit coverage of 95% of the budget between 2019 and 2021.
(c) *Indonesia*: utilizes the Internal Audit Capability Model to assess and monitor the maturity level of internal audit units across the government, with a target for 85% to reach Level 3 capabilities by 2025.
(d) *Kiribati*: An internal audit charter sets out standards and procedures consistent with international best practices, and there is a risk-based annual plan that covers not only central ministries but also extends to outer islands and overseas missions.
(e) *Kyrgyz Republic*: a Strategic Plan for Internal Audits is developed for 3 years on the basis of risk assessments. This is updated annually and serves as a basis for the measures laid down by the Internal Audit Service for full and effective performance of internal audit tasks.
(f) *Maldives*: professionalization of the internal audit function is done through the adoption of the International Professional Practice Framework for Internal Auditing, and introduction of the Audit Information System model.
(g) *Mongolia*: the MOF in 2019 approved a Quality Assurance Methodology on internal audit in line ministries.
(h) *Philippines*: developed the Philippine Government Internal Audit Manual and the Internal Auditing Standards for the Philippine Public Sector to promote effective and ethical operations across all internal audit units.

Auditing[57]

Three particular issues are central on auditing: (a) independence of the agency carrying out the functions, (b) coverage and standards that govern the audits, and (c) legislative scrutiny of the audit reports. One of the primary features of an effective audit system is its **independence** (both organizational, i.e., from the executive; and financial,

[57] This refers to external auditing, distinct from internal audit provisions which agencies in the executive branch are responsible for. External auditing is carried out by an independent Supreme Audit Institution in the country.

i.e., resourcing provided outside the government's budgeting system, and therefore, not in the government's control).[58] Effective auditing is then carried out by an SAI (e.g., the COA) which operates independently with unrestricted and timely access to all required information.

A common concern regarding the independence of SAIs across DMCs is their dependence on the executive branch for the approval of their budget. For instance, in the Republic of the Marshall Islands (RMI), the Office of the Auditor General needs to obtain executive approval for its budget and lacks a direct appeal to the legislature if resources are insufficient. Although some SAIs, like the Mongolian National Audit Office, submit their budget directly to the legislature, the MOF may still amend the proposal during its integration into the national budget. The Auditor General's Office in Maldives faces operational restrictions on its finances since it needs MOF approval for large expenditures, travel outside the capital, and staff recruitment/termination, despite constitutional guarantees of independence.

The point on access to information is very critical here. For example, employees of the Chamber of Accounts in the Kyrgyz Republic, in the exercise of their powers, have the right to unlimited access to primary documents reflecting economic and financial activities, financial registers, balance sheets and accounts, and other information necessary for auditing. In Maldives, the Audit Act provides powers to the Auditor General's Office to have access to all records, books, vouchers, documents, receipts, cash, stamps, securities, goods, or any other items, and may make copies of such documents in the performance of its functions.

In the work of the SAI, **audit coverage and standards** are also relevant to note. The central plank here is on its focus on material issues and systemic and control risks in government agencies, all based on national auditing standards that are aligned to the International Standards of Supreme Audit Institutions. The term "material issues" reflects the need for the SAI to look at, for example, performance-related issues more than administrative/compliance or even financial ones. One relevant standard is on taking a risk-based approach to audits which enables the SAI to target areas where there are risks to the government of improper transactions. As for coverage, this includes the state's public accounts, the management of public funds and state-owned assets, and all transactions involving public funds or property. Several SAIs (for example, those in Pakistan and Solomon Islands) have also ventured into auditing SDGs.

The audit reports are then submitted for **legislative scrutiny**. For the reports to be effective, they will need to be scrutinized by the legislative branch, generally the Public Accounts Committee (PAC), which will concentrate on the execution of the approved budget as documented in the SAI reports. Still, the PAC can only look at how public money was spent and accounted for, not the merits of the underlying policy.

Also, there are generally time lags in such reviews. In Bangladesh, for example, the most recent audit reviewed by the PAC and published on the external website is for FY2017/18, that is, a time lag of 8 years at least. In Maldives, the PAC has a significant backlog due to the volume of reports submitted, with about 700 reports alone in 2023. This highlights the value of a risk-based approach to audit reviews as its absence, seen in the above examples, results in a significant caseload of audit scrutiny work.

[58] The situation on financial (in)dependence of the SAI to the executive can be seen in the Philippines. The Commission on Audit (COA) enjoys fiscal autonomy under the Constitution, which mandates its approved annual budget to be automatically and regularly released. Although the COA's budget is included in the General Appropriations Act, which is subject to legislative scrutiny prior to approval, there has been no reported instance of restriction placed on COA budget or funds flow.

Reporting

Three main aspects of reporting that can be highlighted as part of the PFM system are highlighted: annual, in-year, and their summative implications for fiscal transparency.[59] In order for the audit exercise to be effective and thorough, the complete and consolidated year-end financial statements (i.e., **annual reports**) should be prepared and submitted for external audit. Financial reports contain details of revenue, expenditure, cash flow, short- and long-term liabilities, and financial and nonfinancial assets. The last component is something that is not very robust in many DMCs; indeed, it is not unusual to find incomplete or outdated fixed assets registers.

There is a very specific reason why the annual reports need to show comparisons with the approved budget: this allows the government to ensure compliance with the ex-ante specification of the budget as approved by the legislature. The annual report is compared with the approved budget and contains information on a range of variables such as revenues, expenditures, and assets.

The reporting standards adopted by a DMC, particularly the extent to which its national standards align with international ones such as the IPSAS, and the adoption of the International Financial Reporting Standards (IFRS) for its statutory bodies, are not necessarily symbiotic. As evidenced in Mongolia, the central government follows a modified IPSAS while SOEs follow the IFRS, and a key challenge in adopting an accrual-based IPSAS is how to incorporate financial reports of SOEs into the government's consolidated financial reporting.

Governments will also need to regularly report (i.e., **in-year reporting**) on budget execution (which includes revenue and expenditure data) so as to enable performance monitoring and maintain (or adjust) planned budget outturns. In preparing a monthly report on budget implementation, it is preferable to include a commentary and analysis on budget execution (as is done, for example, by the Kyrgyz Republic Treasury). The commentary that is provided will be helpful in making sense of the context of the evidence presented.

Both in-year and annual reports of a government's financial activities are inherently tied to information on its fiscal plans, positions, and performance that is easily available to the public. This transparency is said to be low in DMCs where key budget documents or information are limited in availability or delayed in publication (for example, the Federated States of Micronesia's reports omit commitment data, while the RMI only publishes execution data, thereby limiting the usefulness of financial information for decision-making and mid-year course correction).

On the other hand, enacted budgets and audited financial statements tend to be published when there is a growing recognition of the importance of fiscal transparency (such as in Kiribati, Georgia, and the Philippines, to name a few). To ensure fiscal transparency, governments also release macroeconomic forecasts and simplified budget summaries following legislative approval. These practices reflect a gradual strengthening of transparency mechanisms, despite variations in coverage and timing. Georgia exercises several good practices in fiscal transparency, as shown in **Box 7**.

Procurement

With a considerable amount of funds spent on procurement by governments (in Viet Nam, for example, almost 40% of GDP), this has been one of the most critical governance- and PFM-related issues across all DMCs.[60] Some of the core principles that underlie the function of public procurement include those of: (a) value for

59 The discussion on fiscal transparency is highlighted in the following section on Managing Fiscal Risks, given the close associative relationship between transparency of reporting (or the lack thereof) and the fiscal risks that emerge out – or that are symptomatic – of the non-transparency.

60 Indeed, procurement-related corruption cases are also not insignificant. In Maldives, for example, data from the Anticorruption Commission in 2022 showed that almost a third of the 486 cases registered with the Commission were on procurement (https://acc.gov.mv/en/publications/184; accessed 11 August 2025).

Box 7. Good Practices in Fiscal Transparency in Georgia

In Georgia, the following types of budgetary information are publicly available:

(a) Annual executive budget proposal documentation together with the supporting documentation and within the timeframe established by the law is available on the MOF website on the dates of submission of the proposal to the government and the legislature by the MOF.
(b) Enacted annual budget – made available to the public on the MOF website from the date of its approval by the legislature.
(c) In-year budget execution reports – quarterly reports are submitted to the legislature together with supporting documentation and materials within one month from the completion of the quarter.
(d) Annual budget execution report – covering the execution of revenues, expenditures and balances of the State budget, the budgets of the Autonomous Republics and local self-governing units are all available to the public on the website of the MOF immediately after their submission to the legislative body.
(e) Audited annual financial report, incorporating or accompanied by the external auditor's report.
(f) Pre-budget statement – Government approves the country's Basic Data and Directions Document each year.
(g) Other external audit reports – the State Accounting Office (SAO) prepares a report on spending execution in line ministries. It also issues various reports on public sector performance, and the annual report on the activity of the Audit Office. All reports of the SAO are available on its website as soon as they are issued.
(h) Summary of the Budget proposal or enacted budget. MOF has been preparing an annual Citizen's Guide to the State Budget Law since 2012. This document is prepared for both the draft budget and the approved budget: the draft Citizen Budget is updated as soon as the approved Budget is published and is made available immediately on the website of the MOF. Since 2016, the report has also been published and sent to spending institutions, as well as to development partners and NGOs.
(i) Macroeconomic forecasts – Information on these forecasts is part of the annual Basic Data and Directions Document that is updated regularly until its final endorsement (July 10 of each year) and is made immediately available in the MOF website at each update stage.

Source: Country diagnostic work for the Georgia CPS, 2023.

money; (b) uniformity (such that procurement systems are not fragmented across different agencies); and (c) efficiency (e.g., that derived from bulk purchasing or from framework contracts, and also that focus on a whole-of-government approach to procurement).

Any review of public procurement should encompass (1) legislative and regulatory frameworks, (2) institutional framework and management capacity, (3) procurement operations and market practices, and (4) accountability, integrity, and transparency. Also of interest is the emerging consideration of sustainable public procurement.

(1) Legislative and regulatory frameworks

The focus here is on whether the laws and regulations that govern procurement align with internationally recognized principles and obligations. Most DMCs have dedicated laws that govern public procurement; some, such as Bhutan, have procurement operations that are governed by subsidiary legislation of the Financial Management Act, or the Public Finance Act, or similar regulations. While having public procurement regulations as a subsidiary legislation allows easier amendments, the fact that regulations can be changed by administrative fiat without parliamentary involvement or approval introduces an uncertain environment for firms. On the other hand, some jurisdictions that have dedicated procurement legislation may find it challenging to address changes in industry practices, such as those that hinder value for money in public procurement due to provisions that limit competition.

The recent procurement reforms adopted by Mongolia and Georgia illustrate how DMCs can balance stability and adaptability by combining principle-based legislation with comprehensive secondary regulations. In Mongolia, the 2024 Public Procurement Law is comprehensive and includes provisions such as for life-cycle cost estimation as well. Secondary regulations are also clear and comprehensive. In Georgia, the 2023 Public Procurement Law delineates new public procurement procedures ensuring prudent and efficient use of public funds in procurement contracts. The law is widely perceived as progressive by the NGO sector as it clearly spells out potential conflicts of interest scenarios including in relation to subcontractors. The law introduces transparent rules for complaints management and the selection of the Dispute Resolution Board members equipping them with a high degree of independence.

(2) Institutional framework and management capacity

The main point is whether the public procurement system is mainstreamed and well-integrated with the PFM system in the country. Across all DMCs, budget allocations are known a few months in advance of the budget year, which allows for adequate procurement planning. Moreover, advance procurement activities are possible for agencies that follow the Procurement Regulations and those with special arrangements. In DMCs where there is no formal procurement manual to assist procurement practitioners, such as Maldives, there are some constraints on procuring entities.

Most jurisdictions (such as Kazakhstan and the Lao PDR) have their procurement policy and regulatory functions under the MOF or a unit directly reporting to it. In others, such functions are exercised by institutions operationally independent from the MOF. The National Public Procurement Agency in Indonesia, the Public Procurement Regulatory Authority in Pakistan, and the Government Procurement Policy Board in the Philippines are some examples that are involved in regulation and oversight, policy and framework development, capacity-building, and electronic government procurement (e-GP) operations (indeed, the e-procurement portal is a core part of the institutional framework on procurement). They also formulate appropriate procurement policies and conduct compliance assessment of procurement functions and activities across the whole of government.

Professional development opportunities on procurement are generally not available across the DMCs, and there appears to be a clear lack of a professionalization program that will continually improve the capacity of procurement practitioners (even though some DMCs, such as Fiji, have a clearly defined procurement competency framework). Bangladesh has a comprehensive training program featuring a three-week modular training course as the core training, linked to advanced training and academic programs such as the Chartered Institute of Procurement and Supply courses. In DMCs where such systems are lacking (e.g., Turkmenistan), the general trend has been to rely on learning on-the-job. **Box 8** indicates some good practices on management capacity enhancement in procurement in Indonesia.

Generally, ***management capacity gaps on public procurement*** in DMCs have been oft-cited in the Methodology for Assessing Procurement Systems reports.[61] In developing professional programs on building capacity for public procurement, three specific components will need to be considered: (a) a high-level orientation program to be provided for heads of agencies and departments; (b) a technical training program to be provided for operations staff; and (c) a specialized e-procurement module to be developed to acquaint users of the system. More broadly, DMCs have generally opted to put in place reforms on public procurement in a sequential manner, which enables them to take a more structured approach to bedding in the reforms before higher-level reforms are considered. **Table 3** lists the experience of Nepal in this regard.

[61] Methodology for Assessing Procurement Systems is a universal tool to evaluate public procurement systems across countries. It is a joint initiative of the World Bank and OECD, and is based on comprehensive indicators on legislation, regulation, policies, institutional framework, management capacity, market practices, and integrity framework related to public procurement.

Box 8. Good Practices in Management Capacity in Procurement, Indonesia

Substantive efforts have been made to professionalize the public procurement profession. There is recognition of procurement as a profession with the status of civil servants, with competency standards set for public procurement functional positions. Further, provisions on "Training for Procurement" establish the details of accreditation and training programs.

Based on feedback from the Indonesian Procurement Experts Association, the national public procurement agency (*Lembaga Kebijakan Pengadaan Barang-Jasa Pemerintah* [LKPP]) has developed a structured training program based on competency standards for government procurement officers. There is a clear appointment procedure with some standard credit points for professional development. The implementation of a robust certification program ensures that the procurement process is run by qualified personnel.

Source: country diagnostic work for the Indonesia CPS, 2024.

Table 3. Proposed Actions on Public Procurement Reforms, Nepal

For immediate action	For the medium term	For the long term	For continual action
• Timely updating of the PPA and PPR • Make e-GP more effective by, for example, incorporating provisions for profiles of those seeking tenders • Organizational reforms within PPMO • Priority action on requirements specified in the PPA on, for example, guidelines, processes, standard bidding document templates, etc. • Training for all officials involved in public procurement across all three levels of government to develop their skills in this area • Develop a code of conduct (related to public procurement) for public officials and those in private sector	• Permanent platform for procurement specialists to interact on • Institutional capacity building of PPMO (including of full staff complement)[a] • Align the objectives of mid-term plans, MTEF, procurement plans, and budgets (particularly how the plans and budgets will deliver the results)	• e-GP to be used for all public procurement to ensure transparency and effectiveness • Procurement action to be carried out only by qualified procurement specialists	• Make procurement monitoring regular and effective • Strategic focus for each stage of public procurement • Regular research on public procurement issues • Continued efforts of all parties in public procurement to adhere to a code of conduct

e-GP = electronic government procurement; MTEF = medium-term expenditure framework; PPA = Public Procurement Act; PPMO = Public Procurement Monitoring Office; PPR = Public Procurement Regulations.

[a] Vacancy rate in 2024/25: 4.5% (or two vacancies out of 44 mandated positions); in 2022/23, this was 18%.

Source: *PPMO Annual Report, 2082* (2024/25), p. 58.

(3) Procurement operations and market practices

Procuring entities in DMCs conduct needs analysis and market research, in varying degrees, to guide the development of their procurement requirements. In Fiji, for example, there are some manual monitoring and spend analysis exercises to identify high-impact areas for establishing the whole-of-government procurement under a framework agreement. The proposed amendments to the Procurement Regulations seek to introduce a strategic procurement planning process. Framework agreements are not uniformly used in operations across DMCs, however.

As for practices related to market development, in DMCs such as Cambodia, there is strong consideration being given to legally limit the use of single source procurement by introducing additional criteria to avoid inappropriate use and, as a result, encourage more competitive procedures. In Turkmenistan, there are some restrictions on the nationality of bidders (e.g., if there are enough potential bidders in the domestic market, then the procuring entity has the right to limit participation to domestic bidders, or to prioritize state enterprises and/or public organizations of people with disabilities). Where goods are produced in the country, the procuring entity may limit the list of bidders to domestic small and medium-sized enterprises and/or may establish conditions for use of local raw materials.

The importance of preparing rigorous cost estimates for purposes of effective procurement cannot be overstated. This is a serious issue in some DMCs (such as Azerbaijan) because cost estimates may eventually be posted as the ceiling for contract awards (which means that bids above the ceiling will be rejected). While there may be encouragement to use broader market information, procuring entities may not be doing this consistently. In DMCs where there are no written or formal procedures for the preparation of cost estimates to ensure adequacy and accuracy before bidding, each agency will tend to follow its own guidelines.

The inherent weaknesses in procurement operations in DMCs can best be highlighted through detailed data analysis carried out by the World Bank of public procurement transactions for 2013–2016 in Georgia. The evidence may be dated, but the results are illuminative (**Box 9**).

Box 9. Results of Analysis of Public Procurement Transactions in Georgia (2013–2016)

The World Bank found the following about public procurement transactions in the country:

Type of procurement	Levels of contract (Max. value of $2,000)	Accounting for share of total spending
Goods & services	~ 90%	> 10%
Civil works	~ 45%	~ 1%

The conclusion was that, overall, the bulk of time and effort in public procurement is devoted to processing very small transactions, which is highly inefficient. Also, although the proportion of simplified procurement declined during the period, in 2016, this method still accounted for 88% of all contracts and 30% of total contract value.

As per the World Bank report, data on the failure rate of procurement opportunities that went through e-tendering were concerning. Over the 4-year period, an average of 29.1% of e-tenders did not result in a signed contract. This average remained relatively constant over the period, with some decline in 2016 and 2017 (about 27% of e-tenders failed). Also, the average number of bids for open tenders did not surpass three in any year (i.e., competition had been minimal). Other findings included wide performance variations between civil works procuring entities, and the need for improving procurement data analysis within the State Procurement Agency.

Several reasons were named for these results, including no wider announcement, insufficient procurement planning, and possible collusion between companies.

Source: ADB's country diagnostic work for the Georgia CPS, 2023, citing Turkewitz, et al, 2018.

(4) Accountability, integrity, and transparency

Considerations of *accountability, integrity, and transparency* in procurement are important and have increasingly garnered attention across DMCs. This is particularly so since corruption and mismanagement issues feature prominently in the public procurement domain.

Various elements can be specified here that go to the heart of enhancing integrity in the public procurement system, the ones with the possibility of greater impact being: (a) a robust procurement code of conduct; (b) clear supplier debarment conditions; and (c) an open and effective grievance redress system which has features such as remedies for suppliers, complaints filing, and impartial hearing procedures. Evidence of this last element, such as in Georgia, appears to be an absolute must for demonstrating credible commitment to integrity in the public procurement system.

Accountability and integrity issues in public procurement also extend to contract management and monitoring systems. Such systems are in place in most DMCs, even if rudimentary for some. There are provisions in place to check that contracts are implemented in a timely manner, and inspections are carried out even if they may be sporadic.

Some of the weaknesses in procurement operations that are evident in Nepal undermine efforts at enhancing integrity in the public procurement system. These weaknesses include: (a) slicing (i.e., fragmentation of large contracts), packaging (aggregation of smaller contracts), and preparing specifications to contracts that are aligned to only a particular firm, thus limiting competition; (b) inaccurate application of the procurement law; (c) lack of due diligence prior to issuing contracts; and (d) ghost contracting in joint ventures where the foreign partner (usually the stronger entity) is missing in contract execution.

Sustainable Public Procurement

An emerging theme in this space is that **of sustainable public procurement (SusPP),** something not comprehensively referenced in the procurement domain across all DMCs. SusPP has been gaining momentum as a core value-based way of carrying out procurement, and where emphasis is on, among others: (a) organization governance (including decision-making processes); (b) labor practices (including employee protection); (c) environmental impact (including focus on climate, pollution, and biodiversity); and (d) fair operating practices (including anticorruption and fair competition). It is this comprehensiveness of coverage that makes SusPP so holistic in how procurement can contribute to national development objectives.

Globally, based on the United Nations Environment Programme data collection exercise for SDG 12.7.1, Asia and the Pacific is at a medium to low level of SusPP implementation, with all eight reporting countries from the region showing some form of integration of sustainability requirements or both sustainability requirements and eco-labels in procurement.[62]

Indonesia's experiences in SusPP are detailed in **Box 10**.

[62] UNDP. n.d. *Progress on Sustainable Public Procurement Implementation: Preliminary Insights of SDG 12.7.1 2025 Data Collection Exercise* (accessed 27 January 2026).

Box 10. Sustainable Public Procurement in Indonesia

As part of the government's national policy objectives for sustainable development its procurement legal and regulatory framework provides a good foundation for sustainable public procurement (SusPP).

The application of sustainability criteria is to ensure value for money requiring consideration of sustainability in three aspects in the planning/budgeting process and the preparation of technical specifications, draft contracts, and bidding documents:

- *Economic* (*e.g.,* life cycle costing),
- *Social* (*e.g.,* empowerment of small businesses and gender responsiveness), and
- *Environmental* (*e.g.,* reduction of negative impacts on health and use of natural resources).

High-level information on – and a roadmap for the implementation of – SusPP has been made public; and the government has issued several documents that operationalize SusPP (including guidance notes on sustainable procurement, and standard bidding documents for the procurement of construction works and recruitment of consulting services with sustainable procurement provisions).

Source: Country diagnostic work for Indonesia CPS, citing ADB's 2024 procurement assessment report for the Ministry of Public Works and Housing.

Public Investment Management Systems[63]

(1) Public investment management (PIM) and PFM

The focus on PIM in the discussion on public financial and expenditure management (including public procurement) is not tangential; indeed, there is very clear and consequential linkage. In order to achieve its development objectives, a government will put in place a robust public investment plan that will be subject to the existing PFM system in the country since issues of resources, budgeting, and financial management are central to manage public investments.

At the core of proper PIM is the concept of infrastructure governance, basically strong institutions to manage public investments (the term, refers not only to organizations but also to 'rules of the game' that encompass procedures and conventions on how effective PIM should be achieved). Such an effective PIM has three pillars – planning the investment, allocating resources for the investment, and implementing the investment programs. Overarching these pillars are three cross-cutting requirements of robust ICT systems, a tight legal framework, and enhanced staff capacity. The 'rules of the game' for effective PIM can include, for example: (a) proper monitoring of public assets; (b) proper oversight; (c) alternative infrastructure financing provisions; and (d) strong coordination across all relevant institutions.

(2) PIM practices in DMCs

Some main conclusions on the practice of PIM in developing countries and emerging economies, as drawn from public reports, are worth mentioning here (these conclusions are also generic across the DMCs covered in this study).

63 Public investment management assessments for various DMCs covered in this study are not all in the public domain. Discussions here are stylized to cover the general conclusions reached in various reports.

(a) Institutional design is superior to actual effectiveness in infrastructure governance (i.e., the actions are better on paper than in practice).
(b) Continuing in this vein, with respect to the three pillars of PIM (i.e., planning, allocation, and implementation) in the public investment cycle, allocation of resources and implementation of infrastructure programs and projects score the lowest; planning scores, not surprisingly, tend to be the highest.
(c) This is understandably particularly true for low-income developing countries, which reflect weak implementation capacity.
(d) Finally, institutions specific to public investment (e.g., project appraisal, project selection, and maintenance funding) are less efficient than the more general PFM institutions (such as fiscal targets and rules).

Five main provisions are critical for strong PIM: (a) close links among the public investment plan, the medium-term fiscal and expenditure frameworks, and the annual budget; (b) clear guidelines, for preparation, appraisal, prioritization, and approval of projects to direct and guide future front-end investment processes;[64] (c) particular focus on a well-resourced operations and maintenance budget for all investment-related agencies; (d) strong provisions and processes for asset management;[65] and (e) robust monitoring protocols for investment projects.

One particular dimension to note is that of the role of SOEs in public investments, and more importantly, their generally weak contribution to proper PIM. In several DMCs, for example, SOEs have a significant role in public investment, yet the governance and oversight framework are deemed insufficient. There is also a lack of clarity regarding the roles and responsibilities of related ministries and agencies, which poses a risk of duplication.[66]

(3) Attributes of a weak PIM system

Across DMCs where the PIM system is weak, the following attributes are generally evident: (a) fragmentation among the proposals of the public investment program, particularly when they are governed by different regimes, depending on the funding source; and (b) the absence of a single rigorous framework for selecting and screening investment projects in use across all government agencies.

The latter condition is compounded when the methodology for ensuring that all planned projects follow basic minimum criteria (such as minimum social rates of return) is not rigorously adhered to. The results of such weaknesses are invariably that there is a lack of coherence between investment projects and national strategic development objectives, between current and investment components of the budget, and between national and regional investment objectives. **Table 4** shows these weaknesses across the various stages of PIM.

Efforts are being made by DMCs to address these weaknesses. In Cambodia, for example, the 2023 PIMA recommended stronger coordination of investment planning between levels of government, development of a much stronger maintenance policy framework, and coordination of public investment management information technology development. In the Kyrgyz Republic, there are regulations in place that all new investment proposals are subject to economic analysis. Externally financed investment projects require the approval of the Council on Fiscal and Investment Policy.

The experiences of Georgia show some good practices in PIM that are relevant to highlight here (**Box 11**).

64 These guidelines include screening tools for evaluating the economic impact, climate and disaster risk, and social impact of public investment proposals.

65 Provisions for public asset management have not been emphasized across the DMCs to the extent they should be. Efforts, such as the Public Asset Management System in Nepal, are noteworthy. There are still lapses in the system but better accounting of public assets by the federal and subnational governments (provincial as well as local) is welcome.

66 The matter of ineffective SOEs is provided in the section on Managing Fiscal Risks.

Table 4. Attributes of Weak Public Investment Management Systems at Various Stages

PIM Stage	Observed Weaknesses across DMCs
Planning	1. National and sectoral strategies not effectively guiding public investment decisions due to inconsistencies in project information and absence of resource envelope constraints 2. For the multi-year investment plan and budget, not seeking to ensure full cost disclosure (project costs as well as lifecycle costs) in budget documents; future recurrent costs not being rigorously calculated 3. Limitations in economic analysis of proposals and in project selection 4. Absence of robust project appraisal systems, including application of a standard methodology, and a weak capital project selection process
Allocation	1. Little or no power of the MOF to reprioritize projects that overspend (which undermines the reliability of the MTEF) 2. Lack of a medium-term capital budget ceiling as part of a binding resource envelope for ministries at the start of the annual budget process 3. Funds allocations for capital projects are not credible due to non-binding appropriations 4. No centralized project pipeline or selection criteria for major projects, and projects are selected based on the availability of financing rather than project viability
Implementation	1. The e-procurement system not well-integrated with the government FMIS 2. Weak project management arrangements (e.g., sector ministries not appointing a senior project manager to ensure successful project preparation and implementation) 3. Project management weakened by the absence of a formal methodology to identify tasks, establish accountability, define institutional arrangements, and ensure proactive management 4. Project implementation plans may be modified significantly throughout the year (thus limiting the government's ability to control project implementation) 5. MOF may only be empowered to scrutinize domestically financed projects and may have limited resources and/or mandate to scrutinize and control major, externally financed projects
Monitoring	1. Lack of real-time data 2. Unclear project monitoring procedures; and where they are clear, a general attribute of not rigorously enforcing such procedures 3. Information not incorporated in ongoing reform processes

DMC = developing member country, FMIS = financial management information system, MTEF = medium-term expenditure framework, MOF = ministry of finance, PIM = public investment management.

Source: ADB and various country diagnostic reports.

Box 11. Public Investment Management Practice in Georgia

For developing and implementing Single Cycle Management of capital/investment projects, the following measures are taken at the stages of preliminary and final selection of investment projects:

a. **Preliminary selection and evaluation of projects.** The first stage of the investment project management process involves the development of a project concept card and a preliminary cost-benefit analysis, on the basis of which a decision must be made.

b. **Final evaluation and selection of project.** The decision-making process through project cost-benefit analysis and/or other ways of feasibility studies identified by the Interagency Commission ensures that the project with the highest social and economic results is identified.

continued on next page

Box 11 *continued*

The preparation of the annex of capital projects is part of the budget application and is carried out through the electronic budget management program (eBudget.ge). Projects are published on the MOF website and constitute an important part of the overall state budget documentation. In the case of investment projects prepared by the new regulations (Decree No. 679) guide, current and capital expenditures are separated, and forecasts are made for an average period of 15 years.

Information about the expenditures on investment projects and about the progress of the projects is prepared and reflected in the annual budget report as an annex of capital projects and is available on the MOF website. The annual execution reports have performance indicators related to the implementation of capital projects. For each project there is an initial plan that covers project execution and its financing/payment schedule on a quarterly basis. Monitoring project implementation may use project consultants that report on physical progress that is linked to the invoicing for work completed. For smaller projects, this may be done by an in-house team.

Source: Country diagnostic work for the Georgia CPS, 2023.

Some Key Issues to Note in Public Financial Management and Expenditure Management

Weak legislative framework. Broad observations on the features of, and issues in, public financial and expenditure management systems across the DMCs can begin with weak or inadequate framework legislation that governs intergovernmental fiscal arrangements and relationships and PFM systems across levels of government. This is a vexing issue in federalized government systems, such as Nepal, particularly one that is still in the throes of a political system to which it is very new.

Even in non-federal government systems, it is critical to get the intergovernmental fiscal transfer system right through legal and other provisions that demonstrate to SNGs that there is credible commitment on the part of central government for making the resource transfer process timely and transparently. A fair bit of the transfers takes the form of conditional grants for which framework provisions will need to be clear since these pose hard budget constraints on SNGs.

Inadequate management systems. Weak provisions in the establishment of expenditure and revenue management systems at all levels of government have also adversely impacted improvements in strong public financial and expenditure management. Such an absence has a direct bearing on public expenditure management, and also indeed on information gaps to the public on how public resources are being used.

Evidence of ineffectiveness in capital expenditure performance is also a worrisome development in many countries. In particular, the need to strengthen the link among the broad investment plan, the national development plan, and the infrastructure development plan all within the confines of the annual budget (and keeping in mind the MTEF for public investment) is paramount. Relatedly, there is also a critical need for robust monitoring and evaluation (M&E) systems, databases, and information systems on public financial and expenditure management. Their absence makes implementation of program-based budgeting very difficult.

Public expenditure reviews in many DMCs also show that concerns such as on expenditure arrears, inaccurate registers, embryonic risk management systems, and weak dispute resolution mechanisms, have held back development of effective PFM systems. Also of note is the issue of insufficient capital budget allocation and low budget execution in multi-year contracts.

Public procurement lapses. As discussed earlier, there is an overriding need to substantially strengthen public procurement processes, not so much in the legislative arrangements but in institutional capacity, market practices, and integrity systems. Given the close link between public procurement and the PFM system, this exercise to strengthen the public procurement system cannot come too soon.

Sequenced reforms stand a better chance of success. This practice of sequencing reforms is evident, for example, in Lao PDR where PFM reforms are seen across three phases (**Figure 7**).

Figure 7. Public Financial Management Reform Phases in the Lao People's Democratic Republic, 2005–2030

PHASE I (2005–2017)	PHASE II (2018–2025)		PHASE III (2026–2030)
Legal framework reform; revenue and expenditure centrally managed	***Step 1*** (2015–2020) Put in place financial compliance and fiscal controls for strong PFM core	***Step 2*** (2021–2025) Improve fiscal stability and sustainability	Promote the efficiency and effectiveness in service delivery

Source: ADB country diagnostic work for CPS for the Lao PDR, 2023, citing government sources on public finance development strategy.

Budget credibility. The annual budget will have to be credible, and it will have to be shown to be an integral part of a MTFF. While generally this, in itself, is not a very serious lapse across DMCs, where more attention is needed is in the rigorous application of rules designed to control arrears, and reform procurement processes. Fiscal reporting could also be improved, particularly offering analysis of fiscal risks in a transparent manner.

Effective legislative oversight is the cornerstone of fiscal discipline and public accountability in a democratic system. It ensures that executive branches of government are held responsible for their financial management, particularly in the critical area of expenditure arrears. While the mechanisms for oversight—such as SAIs and PACs—exist on paper, their ability to enforce accountability is frequently undermined by a combination of systemic weaknesses and political realities.

SOE reforms and political will. As SOEs are often at the center of expenditure overloads in developing countries, their reforms occupy the minds of policymakers. SOEs are significant economic actors and critical components of the broader PFM landscape. As they often operate at the intersection of commercial objectives and public policy, their governance, financial reporting, and accountability mechanisms carry unique fiscal risks. The central challenge in SOE reform is not merely technical or financial but fundamentally an issue of governance and political will. Even where formal checks and balances exist—such as corporate governance laws or the requirement to table annual reports in Parliament—they are rendered impotent without the political will to act on them. Thus, having ample opportunity for legislators to take the SOE to task is meaningless if that opportunity is not seized due to political considerations. This failure to enforce consequences is the central obstacle to meaningful SOE reforms, and by extension, broader PFM and expenditure management as well.

Managing Fiscal Risks

Introduction

The issue of fiscal risks is a severe one for most DMCs. All of them have had to tackle them consistently in their PFM systems. Fiscal risks emanate from a variety of factors, including (a) a high degree of contingent liabilities that a government incurs, and for which no provisioning in the budget has been made; (b) disasters emerging from climate-related risks and other natural events, like earthquakes; (c) financial crises that are not of a country's own doing; (d) commodity price shocks; (e) health crises resulting from pandemics (COVID-19 being the most recent example), among others. Fiscal risks need to be very rigorously analyzed and closely monitored. DMCs that have strong institutions and processes, as well as independent oversight, will be able to better manage their fiscal risks.

At the core, fiscal risks are basically "deviations of fiscal outcomes to what was expected at the time of budget formulation."[67] These risks are regarded as being biased towards the downside – in simple terms, a negativity bias, meaning where negative information has a greater impact on government actions to mitigate the risks. This makes sense because fiscal risk realization obviously can be costly, as was evident when the fiscal implications of COVID-19 began to play out, not only with respect to immediate healthcare costs but also to long-term and society-wide interventions that were needed to sustain both the economy and healthcare systems. Indeed, the COVID-19 pandemic was deemed to trigger the largest fiscal risk realization since World War II. And in a way, policy responses to COVID-19 resulted in stressful fiscal risk exposures for many developing countries.

Thus, a better understanding of the nature of these fiscal risks, how they are imposed, what repercussions they will have on the economy (and to society as well), and how they can be better addressed/managed will determine the degree of credibility with which governments demonstrate commitment to their development policies.

Sources of Fiscal Risks

At the core of the notion of fiscal risks are obviously the financial and economic costs of bad policies, natural hazards and man-made, as well as expected and unexpected, and mismanagement of resources. Fiscal risks are aggravated when there are no mitigative measures in place, either by the government (at all levels) or the private sector. These risks may or may not pan out, but it is relevant to specify and articulate clearly and openly how they will be dealt with from a fiscal perspective.

Resulting from SOEs. SOEs play a big role in all economies; indeed, it is estimated that SOEs throughout the world manage public assets equivalent to half of global GDP. While some SOEs in DMCs are stellar, many are not, and governments continue to have significant exposure to these public enterprises, thus bearing potentially huge fiscal risks. In addition, the level of subsidies provided to these entities often far outweighs the dividends and taxes that come from them. Further, there are the more substantive fiscal risks that governments incur from the share of contingent liabilities arising from guarantees they provide to SOEs.

Fiscal risks from SOEs arise from, among others, (a) lower than dividends expected ex-ante; (b) higher levels of subsidies for SOEs to carry on their work, due to weak due diligence; (c) the non-repayment of loans, which is an obvious result for unprofitable SOEs, are not making profits; (d) an increasing need to service the guarantees on their borrowings if conditions so demand; and (e) equity injections to cover previous losses.

[67] R. Odawara. 2025. *Fiscal Risks and their Management – What and Why?* Presentation prepared for World Bank Conference on Climate Fiscal Risks. 24–25 February https://thedocs.worldbank.org/en/doc/ade193d38f1c1e3ba322eb72faa716f5-0080012025/original/1-Fiiscal-Risks-and-Their-Management-Feb15-2025.pdf; (accessed: 4 September 2025).

The performance of SOEs is also, almost universally, poorer than that for private firms that operate in the same space. Take, for example, the state-owned banks in Bangladesh, whose financial performance in comparison to others in the market is subpar, as shown in **Table 5**.

Table 5. Performance of State-Owned Commercial Banks in Bangladesh (2020 and 2024)

	Ratio of Net NPL to Net Total Loans		Expenditure-Income Ratio		Return on Asset		Return on Equity	
	2020	**2024**	**2020**	**2024**	**2020**	**2024**	**2020**	**2024**
SCB	0.003	18.32	83.20	89.24	(1.07)	(0.37)	(29.57)	(11.40)
SB	1.32	1.14	158.10	139.29	(3.01)	(2.54)	(13.85)	(10.08)
PCB	(1.54)	0.77	79.60	79.11	0.70	0.48	10.22	8.75
FCB	(0.56)	(0.50)	46.20	32.35	2.13	4.08	13.10	19.33
Total	**(1.18)**	**3.68**	**79.20**	**80.19**	**0.25**	**0.40**	**4.28**	**7.85**

( ) = negative, FCB = foreign commercial bank, NPL = nonperforming loan, PCB = private commercial bank, SB = specialized bank, SCB = state-owned commercial bank.

Notes:

1. Values are in percent.
2. 2024 data is until end of June.

Source: Bangladesh Bank. 2024. *Annual Report 2023–2024*. Tables 5.03(b), 5.08, and 5.09.

Georgia, on the other hand, is considered to have good practices in place for managing fiscal risks from SOEs (**Box 12**).

Box 12. Managing Fiscal Risks: Georgia's State-Owned Enterprise Strategy

1. MOF has veto power over any investment or borrowing above GEL5 million by any of the large SOEs. The key transformational aspect of this reform is that it puts MOF as the guardian of fiscal risks undertaken by SOEs.
2. SOEs are expected to establish independent supervisory boards with at least two independent members. This helps ensure that only relevant business plans are approved and that SOEs are not entangled in political business cycles.
3. The six largest SOEs are expected to submit Statements of Corporate Intent to MOF annually. This gives MOF an opportunity to dictate limits on profitability, liquidity, and solvency indicators. It also creates a useful platform for SOEs and MOF to discuss their business plans, and capital investment strategies. Most importantly, it creates accountability.

Source: Country diagnostic study for the Georgia Country Partnership Strategy, 2023.

Resulting from PPPs. As governments begin to rely increasingly on partnering with the private sector for resource mobilization, technological systems, and managerial innovations, public–private partnerships (PPPs) gain greater currency as part of formal government policy on any specific sector (although PPPs have been more par for the course in infrastructure sectors where resource requirements are large and often beyond the wherewithal of the government budget). Increasingly, these PPPs have been seen in social sectors as well.[68]

[68] For example, ADB. 2017. PRC: Public–Private Partnerships Demonstration Program to Transform Delivery of Elderly Care Services in Yichang, Hubei (Loan 3506-PRC). The program focused on a pilot delivery of elderly care services in Yichang City, Hubei Province, People's Republic of China, with a total cost of almost $129 million, of which almost 43% was funded by the municipal government, 6% from the private sector, and the rest – 51% – from ADB.

Fiscal risks emerge in PPPs when the government's funding commitment to the project is at risk, such as when the PPP is not be completed on time or if there are cost blowouts (not an unusual occurrence in DMCs), and when governments enter into the PPP agreement without truly appreciating their fiscal implications.[69] The payment of the liabilities that governments incur is the fiscal risk. It is thus recommended that, if governments are keen to emphasize PPPs, they must also establish strong infrastructure governance institutions to manage any associated fiscal risks emanating from them.

Resulting from subnational governments. SNGs face a range of fiscal risks as well, mostly related to expenditure commitments made despite a lack of funding assurances (i.e., implicitly relying on grants and other resource transfers from central government, from which a situation of moral hazard results). One of the ways for central governments to deal with this situation – as evident in, for example, Nepal – is to institute a hard budget constraint on SNGs. Another way to deal with this also is for the central government to use its legislative powers to avert excessive subnational risk-taking (such decision rules are usually inherent in the intergovernmental fiscal framework). To remedy the situation, SNGs, in turn, need to strengthen their capacity to manage their own risks. Clearly, seeking additional own-source revenue measures would help; most SNGs (particularly at the municipal level) are severely constrained in this regard in many countries.

Resulting from standardized guarantees. Quite apart from the guarantees that governments provide to borrowings incurred by SOEs, there are other standardized loans and guarantees (e.g., credit guarantee schemes to facilitate access to finance, or to support small and medium enterprises) that create contigent liabilities to the central government, and which therefore need to be considered as fiscal risks. This may arise if, for example, borrowers default and there are fiscal costs over time.

The IMF's Public Sector Balance Sheet Database shows that the general government loan portfolio averages 6.5% of GDP across a group of 49 countries, and is as large as 20% of GDP in some of them.[70] In and of themselves, loans and guarantees do not have much bearing on the immediate fiscal position since, by definition, they arise only if there is a default down the road, but they do expose governments to substantial fiscal costs downstream.

Contingent liabilities and fiscal risks. These last three sources of fiscal risks (i.e., from SOEs, PPPs, and SNGs) drive home the overall risks emanating from contingent liabilities. While contingent liabilities and other fiscal risks are increasingly being recognized in governments' Economic and Fiscal Update reports, these are not yet being rigorously quantified.[71] This is a common occurrence in many DMCs. Further, there is usually no publicly available information on how the government monitors and reports explicit contingent liabilities from its programs and projects, including those of extrabudgetary units.

Some good practices on reporting contingent liabilities are that records for domestic and foreign debt, including guaranteed debt, are complete, accurate, and updated monthly. These records are reconciled monthly, and comprehensive management and statistical reports covering debt service, stock, and operations are produced and published quarterly. Governments' consolidated financial statements should include reports on contingent liabilities and other fiscal risks, and quarterly debt reports should provide updates on them.

Resulting from climate change impacts, including disasters due to natural hazards. This particular statistic puts this dimension of fiscal risk in stark perspective: there were 23 extreme weather events in the United States in 2023, the total costs of which were more than $57.6 billion.[72] While disasters cannot be forecasted with any degree

69 World Bank. 2022. *Fiscal Risk in PPPs* (accessed 1 August 2025).

70 IMF. 2021a. *Debt Guarantees and Loans Assessment Tool, Fiscal Risks Toolkit* (accessed 27 January 2026).

71 Bova et al. (2016) have indicated that, over 1990–2016, contingent liabilities related to the activity of SOEs and PPPs amounted to around 20% of the total number of materialized contingent liabilities across the countries.

72 The Guardian. 2023. *US Hit by Record Number of Billion-Dollar Climate Disasters*. 11 September.

of certainty, prior investments in resilience planning and capacity to respond swiftly will be positively regarded. The fiscal risks then are inherent in the form of non-investments in proper measures and the costs to pay for such poor planning in the form of repairs, reconstruction, and social welfare and benefits to those affected.

Fiscal risks brought on by climate change may be slow-building, with ample time for governments to make suitable provisions and to put in place both mitigation and adaptation measures. A MTFFcan help incorporate these considerations for purposes of careful fiscal planning. Separately, the formulation of resilience-building policies at all levels of government can help the country better deal with any possible climate change-induced macroeconomic disruptions. What is generally missing is incorporation of information on climate-related liabilities in central government financial reports, and how climate-related management of fiscal risks, debts, and guarantees will be carried out at all levels of government.

Resulting from procurement lapses. There are increasing instances of fiscal risks emanating from lapses in public procurement. Public procurement is a primary area of consideration in any discussion on national development, fiscal risks and PFM systems, and anticorruption measures, among others. It looms large over all projects and national development activities as well as in consideration of consulting services provided to public sector entities across all levels of the governments. How effectively the public procurement system operates will have a strong bearing on ADB portfolio performance in DMCs.[73]

Resulting from poor debt management strategy and practices. A particularly vexing source of fiscal risk stems from improper debt management. As resource needs continue to mount for development works and as resource mobilization (from both domestic and external sources) is not robust, debt levels – and thus correspondingly debt distress – also mount.[74] Across DMCs, annual borrowing must be approved by the legislature, and a medium-term debt management Strategy will include target ranges for indicators for interest rates, refinancing, foreign currency risks, financing strategies, etc. The specific fiscal rules on debt management in Armenia, as shown in **Box 13**, incorporates several internationally recognized good practices.

Need for debt sustainability analysis. The particular issue of relatively poor debt management practices leads to the strong need for a properly carried out debt sustainability analysis (DSA). Governments across the region have carried out such an analysis (or relied on the work of multilateral bodies, such as IMF, to do one), which has been instrumental in giving them proper guidance on how much headroom they may have, and more importantly where severe fiscal risks may emanate if poor debt management continues. **Box 14** provides some information on debt sustainability.

Resulting from miscellaneous sources. Governments are also aware of the need to plan for possible fiscal risks that will be incurred from, for example, an aging population. In DMCs such as the Philippines, where the population of those aged 65 and over is expected to be much higher by 2030, and Nepal where there was an almost 40% increase in older people in 2021 compared to 2011, specific policies are needed to ensure that healthcare, social safety arrangements, and residential care services are planned, and fiscal provisions made accordingly.

[73] It is instructive to consider the case of Nepal here. The 2021 Public Expenditure Review assessment asserted that about 60% of the annual government budget is implemented through procurement; separately, procurement of goods and services accounted for 43% of total spending in 2021 at the provincial and local level. The national budget was NRs1.474 trillion in FY2021/22, 60% of which yields approximately NRs885 billion. Assuming a minimum of 20% reduction in procurement costs through reforms (the lower limit of what is usually argued (see, e.g., IMF, 2023); this amounts to more than NRs176 billion (or $1.3 billion) in nominal savings a year. That such reforms have not taken place can be seen as a fiscal risk of a loss of $1.3 billion.

[74] Debt levels in many countries during the COVID-19 pandemic, for example, remained elevated, and consequent fiscal risks were particularly glaring. Often these led to governments requesting legislative approval to allow for higher debt-to-GDP ratios (as was the case in, among others, Papua New Guinea) by relaxing provisions that may be in place in acts that govern fiscal responsibility.

Box 13. Upgraded Fiscal Rules for Debt Management in Armenia

The amended framework for fiscal rules has four thresholds in Armenia, which can be seen as follows:

IF (Size of Debt)	THEN (Applicable Fiscal Rule)
D > 40% of GDP	• Capital spending should not be below the level of the state budget deficit
D > 50% of GDP	• Previous rule continues to apply, and • Restrictions are imposed on current spending (excluding debt service costs)
D > 60% of GDP	• Previous rules continue to apply, and • Current spending (including debt service costs) cannot exceed the total amount of tax revenue and stamp duties specified in the draft state budget for upcoming year, and • Government must submit a program of measures to the National Assembly to gradually reduce debt to below 60% within a 5-year period
D = 50%–60% of GDP	• Government must design a program of measures in the MTEF to gradually reduce debt to below 50% within a 5-year period

D = debt; GDP = gross domestic product; MTEF = medium-term expenditure framework.
Source: ADB country diagnostic work on Armenia for the CPS, 2021.

Box 14. Observations on Debt Sustainability in Developing Member Countries

In the discussion on public financial and public expenditure systems in DMCs the issue of debt sustainability is a must. In 2022, ADB warned of the dangers that poorer and more vulnerable countries among the DMCs faced, with the need for greater resources counteracted by the need to retain sustainability in the debt situation. There were many messages put forth, the most relevant ones being:

- Problematic composition of a higher level of debt of the lower-income DMCs: more from private lenders, more non-concessional, more foreign currency, and shorter term.
- Many DMCs' capacity to carry public debt is limited, with a similar situation regarding their ability to borrow from private lenders in global financial markets.
- While debt will remain an option as a source of financing, greater priority should be given to, for example, DRM, fiscal retrenchment, structural transformation, etc.
- Also important will be to remove legal, regulatory, and other obstacles to growth, and to construct the pillars of local financial markets.
- Lack of transparency dampens the scope for DMCs to access resources – either internally or externally (but certainly the latter).
- Need to be wary of subnational debt; in countries such as Nepal (where subnational governments are still not at the threshold of borrowing deeply), this is not as serious an issue as, say, Indonesia or the Philippines. Keeping subnational debt sustainable has emerged as an issue in the Upper Middle-Income Countries. Transparency of the fiscal situation would offer some realistic and true-picture status of the debt-sustaining capacity of subnational governments.
- Difficulty in forecasting fiscal accounts. As the PEFA assessment reports of the various DMCs have shown (for indicators on debt management or on forecasting revenues and expenditures), it is asserted that countries regularly miss the forecasted debt ratios and budget balances by a significant margin; it is worse when the forecasted period is 2 or more years out. In this situation, then, forecasting debt sustainability levels and proper arrangements based on them are a difficult task.
- Finally, the risk of contingent liabilities impinges directly on debt sustainability. As long as DMCs do not get a good handle on these liabilities, it remains a tall order to speak optimistically of debt sustainability.

Source: Ferrarini, et al. 2022: 7–20.

Fiscal risks can also emerge from governmental policy actions which may not have gone through a due diligence exercise, and for which also the unintended consequences may not have been rigorously thought through. These lead to what are known as 'fiscal cliffs'. In many DMCs, numerous 'white elephant' projects have exposed governments to significant fiscal risks. In addition, policy decisions (such as tax cuts) can also be potential sources of fiscal risks, as is the continued absence of good regulatory frameworks leading to, for example, financial sector instability (e.g., bank failures, resulting from poor supervision).

Measurement of Fiscal Risks

Several measures can be used to highlight the source, form, and intensity of fiscal risks. The repertoire of such measures is deemed adequate in order to sense from where some of the most egregious fiscal risks could emanate. The IMF and World Bank have several tools for measurement that are widely used (**Table 6**).

Table 6. Some Tools to Measure Fiscal Risks

	Tool	Explanation
1	SOE Stress Test	A forward-looking assessment of the resilience of an SOE's financial position and the potential impacts on public finances[a]
2	Fiscal Risk Assessment Tool	Provides a high-level portfolio perspective on risks that governments are usually exposed to. This provides the governments with the most important sources of fiscal risks that they need to take into account in their macrofiscal considerations
3	Debt Guarantee and Loan Assessment Tool	Analyzes loans or explicit debt guarantees to support debt raised by a public or private sector. It helps inform the decision to issue a guarantee or provide a loan as well as support the management of the loan and guarantee portfolios
4	Standardized Guarantees Assessment Tool	IMF's standardized guarantees assessment tool helps countries to assess the fiscal costs and fiscal risks associated with government standardized guarantee schemes, which also helps in monitoring the risks

SOE = state-owned enterprise.

[a] New Zealand's experiences on the application of SOE stress tests are noteworthy. These tests refer to financial resilience assessments for these public companies to assess their vulnerability to serious economic shocks (of the type that was brought on, for example, by COVID-19). These vulnerabilities could be the result of pandemics, exogenous economic shocks and geopolitical events, internal political turmoil, and the like. SOEs are then required to have in place robust risk management protocols to effectively deal with such vulnerabilities.

Source: https://www.imf.org/en/Topics/fiscal-policies/Fiscal-Risks (accessed 4 August 2025).

Management of Fiscal Risks

Evidence shows that proper management of fiscal risks will be based on several measures:

(a) Reliable and comprehensive information and evidence; the data should be trackable, on an ongoing and uniform basis, to capture all aspects of the disasters and their fiscal implications.[75] The data should also be cumulative of the efforts of all agencies and SNGs so that a complete picture emerges.

(b) Comprehensive analysis of the evidence collected so that meaningful reports emerge which give an accurate picture of what contingencies the government will need to plan for by way of spending decisions (e.g., for repair, reconstruction, and social support).

[75] The practices in New Zealand of maintaining a register of national risks are worthwhile for DMCs to assess for applicability. The National Risk Register is a key part of the National Risk and Resilience Framework, and is used to identify, track, and ultimately build resilience to national risks (of which there are currently 28 specified, including risks such as those resulting from adverse weather, disease outbreaks, environmental changes, disruption in trade regimes and financial mechanisms, failures in critical infrastructure, etc.). Obviously not every major risk is captured in the register but for those that are, the government makes targeted decisions to focus resources where they will have the biggest fiscal and human impact. See, for example, https://www.dpmc.govt.nz/our-programmes/risk-and-resilience/national-risk-and-resilience-framework/new-zealands-national-risks (accessed 2 January 2026).

(c) Budget proactively[76] so that the exercise is not a post-event action which often results in claw-backs from all types of budget line items, but rather is something that the government has considered *ex-ante* and made necessary budgetary provisions for and knows exactly what should be clawed back from where.
(d) Public disclosure (i.e., fiscal transparency) so as to ensure proper public accountability; this degree of fiscal transparency is a necessary and sufficient condition to ensure that any emerging fiscal risk, and its response by the government, is well understood by the public and others (see **Box 15** for an example of good practice on this front).
(e) Proper monitoring systems that enable a constant check on the possible impact on fiscal risks the country may face.
(f) Proper assessment at the very beginning of understanding the full extent of obligations in, for example, PPP projects.[77] And once that is determined, then to have strong infrastructure governance institutions in place to manage any fiscal risks.

Box 15. Good Practice in Fiscal Transparency

An evaluation of fiscal transparency in Armenia carried out by the IMF in 2019 found that even as there were a few areas for possible improvement many elements of sound fiscal transparency practices were also evident, such as:

- Publication of a monthly budget execution report within a month comprising multiple classifications;
- Presentation of the annual budget and MTEF with comprehensive macro-economic forecasts, fiscal objectives, and performance information, submitted to the National Assembly in a timely manner;
- Analysis of the impact of alternative macroeconomic scenarios of public finances and fiscal risk disclosure on specific fiscal risks in different documents; and
- Semi-annual monitoring reports on the financial performance of most public corporations, including transfers between government and the corporations.

Source: IMF. 2019.

Creating a more robust and proactive fiscal risk management framework requires taking a forward-looking perspective and emphasizing that technical rules alone are insufficient. Sustainable resilience requires deep institutional capacity, transparent processes, and a more strategic alignment between national governments and international partners. Beyond passively managing existing risks, a forward-looking strategy involves actively improving a country's financial standing. And effective fiscal risk management requires a multi-faceted approach that combines strong internal rules, deep systemic governance reforms, and a conscientious, capacity-aware partnership with international donors.

Reporting Fiscal Risks

Reporting requirements in PFM that dwell on the nature of the fiscal risks the government may be incurring are crucial and carry considerable weight. The focus here is on reports that examine risks arising from public corporations (i.e., SOEs), SNGs, and PPPs. As governments have an oversight role in relation to these entities, reports on fiscal risks (including those that relate to contingent liabilities) become important to them in their monitoring role.

[76] This can be done only if there is evidence on spending projections and historical trends to inform funding amounts.

[77] The PPP Fiscal Risk Assessment Model is used increasingly to better understand the long-term fiscal implications of an individual or a portfolio of projects. The analytical tool helps in the specification and quantification of macrofiscal implications of PPPs. This helps relevant agencies appreciate the fiscal risks assumed by government, and more importantly identify potential mitigation measures.

Some examples are worth mentioning here. In Georgia, a report on all central government contingent liabilities, including their quantification, and other fiscal risks is submitted to Parliament annually and published. It covers information/analysis on risks by public corporations, quasi-fiscal activities, PPPs, and other risks such as from pandemics, disasters and climate change.[78] In the Philippines, this is adequately audited and reported by the COA which publishes a separate Annual Financial Report for SOEs and for local governments. For both, the report provides essential information on their financial condition, financial performance, net equity, cash flows, budget utilization, and audit results.[79]

Some Key Issues to Note on Fiscal Risks

Vulnerable PFM processes. A review of the incidence of fiscal risks across several DMCs, as well as practices to address them, has flagged a few issues. To begin with, countries with a high fiduciary risk environment demonstrate major weaknesses in budget classification, transparency of intergovernmental fiscal relations, oversight of fiscal risks of public sector entities, and the extent of unreported government operations. Risks also emanate from vulnerable PFM processes leading to uneven pace of expenditures (largely capital since recurrent expenditures are less prone to such unevenness).

In general, a ***weak accounting system*** is not able to provide a fair, accurate, and timely picture of public finances, which is compounded by: (a) ineffective internal controls, audit, and monitoring and evaluation systems; (b) time and quality issues in the auditing system; and (c) low levels of capacity throughout the PFM system.

Poor enforcement of fiscal rules. Formal fiscal rules serve as a primary anchor for fiscal discipline, designed to control deficits, limit spending growth, and maintain debt sustainability.[80] Fiscal indiscipline, however, is a regular concern with fiscal rules poorly enforced and rife financial irregularities, such as bunching of capital expenditure (70% at the end of the fiscal year in some countries). Fiscal indiscipline is also evident in the disconnect between planning and budgeting, poor prioritization of projects and programs, and political influence in project selection. Also relevant is to note a foundational challenge to the efficacy of formal fiscal rules: the selective definition of public debt. By potentially excluding implicit liabilities to meet legal debt ceilings, governments may be creating a facade of fiscal stability while masking the true extent of their risk exposure, thereby undermining the very purpose of the rules. There is thus a critical paradox: while countries have established formal rules to manage fiscal risk, systemic inefficiencies and a narrow definition of public debt can render these frameworks less effective than they are on paper.

[78] Indeed, Georgia attained an open budget index score of 87/100 for transparency in the 2021 as well as the 2023 Open Budget Surveys. It had the highest transparency ranking out of all the countries surveyed in both those years.

[79] This aspect of publishing reports of fiscal risks is at the heart of the focus on transparency in the public sector. In advanced countries, such as New Zealand, for example, PPP contract transparency is one of the core elements of the government's strong drive to ensure good governance. This contract transparency involves guidance from the Treasury, an active role of a dedicated agency on PPP (called the National Infrastructure Funding and Financing Ltd.), and a strong focus on robust processes (including on data sharing and consistent application). Two specific dimensions of this PPP contract transparency are: (a) information sharing on bidder questions and answers with all parties to ensure equal information access; and (b) digital platforms for better procurement data collection with the aim to improve transparency across government procurement, including on PPPs. There are important lessons here for the DMCs that ADB has operations in. For the Treasury's guidance on PPPs, see https://www.treasury.govt.nz/information-and-services/public-sector-leadership/partnerships/public-private-partnerships (accessed 2 January 2026).

[80] Bangladesh, for example, adheres to a key fiscal rule guided by its Public Money and Budget Management Act, which maintains the national budget deficit at a level below 5% of GDP. Further afield from the DMCs considered in this study. Chile's experiences with independent fiscal councils have garnered global attention. The Autonomous Fiscal Council, established in 2019, requires public explanation of fiscal deviations and potential compensation for breaches to maintain fiscal credibility. It has a legal basis and its own budget. This independence in terms of budgetary arrangements, and the fact that its membership is agreed upon by the Senate, gives it a powerful role in terms of instituting adherence by government to specified fiscal rules. Equally significant, it engages with presidential candidates to promote fiscal discipline across different administrations, thus enhancing its credibility and also contributing to Chile's strong governance framework for fiscal management (see, for example, A. Fatas, et al. 2025).

Poor internal control. A high level of fiduciary and corruption risks, particularly in SNGs, as well as inadequate human resources and expertise on PFM is generally evident. This is compounded by poor internal control, and weak enforcement of corrective measures, as well as reporting lapses across the board, evidenced in the regular failure of public enterprises to comply with regulations to submit annual financial statements in relevant line ministries within the stipulated time period.

On fiscal risks emanating from disasters due to natural hazards and climate change vulnerabilities, several climate-responsive PFM Assessments for DMCs have concluded that climate-related management of fiscal risks, debts, guarantees and of non-financial assets is also weak, and climate-risk testing for fiscal risks is still an unexplored area in many DMCs.

In the current uncertain global economic landscape, countries have been encouraged to maintain fiscal discipline, put in place credible medium-term framework and fiscal space, and keep a keen eye out for overarching fiscal risks.[81] When these are then suitably communicated to the public in a transparent manner, managing fiscal risks becomes more facilitated. In that sense, the issue of fiscal transparency thus needs to be mentioned in the same breath while discussing fiscal risks.

Facilitating Private Sector Development

Rationale

It has become axiomatic that governments leveraging the public sector alone will not be able to accelerate sustainable and inclusive economic growth across sectors and regions. Their ambitious goals can only be achieved together with the active participation and engagement of the private sector, which can bring a creative mindset and introduce innovative solutions to spur the economy.

The private sector is the largest contributor to economic growth in developing economies. It generates most quality jobs, contributes to government revenues through the payment of taxes, and introduces innovations that heighten economy-wide efficiency and productivity. However, although a dynamic private sector is vital for the future of Asia and the Pacific, business challenges and financial market gaps still limit its full contribution to economic growth and sustainability.

The United Nations Conference on Trade and Development (UNCTAD) points out that one of the key issues on private sector development (PSD) in developing countries is that they lack medium-sized enterprises, and that the private sector is largely composed of: (a) informal firms; (b) small firms; and (c) microenterprises operating in low value-added sector.[82] With the first group of private sector players (i.e., informal firms), the tax returns are also very minimal since they tend to be outside the tax net even though by UNCTAD estimates this sector alone accounts for around 35% of GDP. For all three, PSD then relies on informed government policies (resulting from extensive consultation and collaboration with the private sector) that directly address built-in constraints and also that foster the creation of small and medium-sized enterprises (SMEs), as well as opportunities to scale them up (since they are not connected well to global value chains). In DMCs, the chambers of commerce always have this preference on the top of their agenda when it comes to interactions with the public sector.

81 IMF. 2025. *Fiscal Monitor*, April, p. x.

82 UNCTAD. 2021. Implementing Supportive Policies to Build a Vibrant Private Sector as a Driver of Structural Transformation. *Policy Brief*, No. 89. October.

The concept of a missing middle that UNCTAD (2020) has articulated in PSD resonates when considering the fact that across many DMCs, only a very few large enterprises dominate the private sector.[83] Hence, UNCTAD has argued that governments need to aggressively develop SMEs so as to narrow the gap inherent in the "missing middle" (between the few large enterprises and the numerous SMEs). This notion of a "missing middle" is clearly evident, in Viet Nam (**Figure 8**).

Figure 8. The "Missing Middle" of Small and Medium-Sized Enterprises in Viet Nam

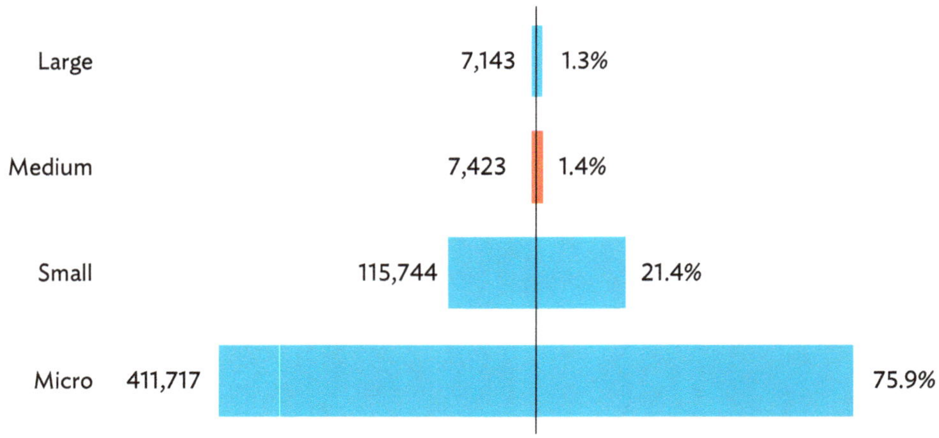

Source: Figure 6: The Missing Middle" – Viet Nam's Enterprise Structure by Size, Inclusive and Sustainable Growth Assessment for the ADB Country Partnership Strategy, 2022–2026, p. 8 (citing General Statistics Office, 2018. Enterprise Survey. Ha Noi).

Constraints the Private Sector Faces

In DMCs where the business environment is generally constrained, this is normally due to the following causes: (a) weak commercial law and regulatory regime (e.g., absence of meaningful legal protection against government expropriation of assets); (b) opaque and onerous bureaucratic processes; (c) endemic corruption; (d) in some DMCs, strict foreign currency controls; (e) poor standards, and practices in, corporate governance (which in itself is hampered by a lack of managerial independence); (f) instances where governments do not fully implement or consistently enforce investment-related legislation; and (g) underdeveloped physical, telecommunications, and other essential infrastructure necessary for businesses to flourish.

Review of the analytical work, country diagnostics work for CPSs, as well as ADB's own investments and technical assistance programs, highlights many constraints in PSD that are echoed elsewhere. Some key constraints include:

(a) Adverse business climate, such as cumbersome administrative rules, and business regulation requirements that are onerous to the private sector.
(b) Related to the business climate, but one that can be separately highlighted, is the culture of unethical practices in the forms of bribery and corruption that are attributes many DMCs exhibit.
(c) Lack of easy access to finance for purposes of business growth.
(d) Difficulty of market access and/or expansion, which often results from well-intentioned but ill-informed policy decisions of governments.

[83] UNCTAD. 2020. *The Least Developed Countries Report 2020: Productive Capacities for the New Decade.* United Nations publication, Sales No. E.21.II.D.2.

(e) An absence of credible commitment to stated policies of governments that creates an environment of unpredictability, an attribute the private sector abhors.
(f) An adverse situation where governments' commitment in DMCs to build appropriate human capital by emphasizing fit-for-purpose technical and vocational education and training is found wanting.[84]

Largely to address these constraints, in 2018, the MDBs Harmonized Framework for Additionality in Private Sector Operations was launched. The principles stipulate that MDBs should: (a) contribute beyond what is available or otherwise absent from the market; (b) catalyze market development and mobilize private sector resources; (c) ensure sustainability of investments, including commercial viability of private sector clients; (d) tackle market failures while minimizing the risk of disrupting or unduly distorting markets; and (e) promote adherence to high standards of conduct in private sector clients.

Across the board, however, the private sector has had issues with the variance in the stated versus revealed preferences of governments towards PSD. An active role for governments to set up the right institutions for the private sector to prosper demonstrates credible commitment on its part to this important public policy imperative.

PPPs as a Core Area of Concern

Specific PSD strands that are evident in the work of governments to support the sector include: (a) creating the right environment (through, e.g., regulatory framework and access to finance); (b) a more robust PPP regime; and (c) targeting macro (i.e., systems level) considerations that impinge on the broad operating environment for the private sector in the economy (e.g., social safeguard requirements that are considered to be too restrictive which generally tend to deter greater private sector involvement). While all three are relevant and important, the focus in this study is on the matter of the PPP regime given its criticality in the emergence of fiscal risks for the economy (see the prior section on Managing Fiscal Risks).

Active cooperation with the private sector and furthering non-state sources of funds based on PPPs are identified by many governments (for example, Turkmenistan) as one of several areas of financing to help implement national development priorities and achieve the SDGs.[85] Generally, areas such as investment programs for industrial and social infrastructure, green economy, and financing of SMEs are mentioned. In Uzbekistan, the rapid expansion of PPP projects is bringing in investment into energy infrastructure, education, health and rural infrastructure such as water supplies. This has been the most effective mechanism for attracting international contractors to work in these sectors.

However, setting up PPPs and incentivizing and engaging with the private sector is a complicated task and includes the participation of several government entities, which demonstrates how complicated the process can really be. **Table 7** puts this in perspective with respect to the situation evident in Kazakhstan.

Moreover, there are also some lapses in terms of access to information that the private sector and others would be interested in. The IMF in 2020[86] highlighted the following data-related lapses with respect to PPPs: (a) no publication of information on assessments of financial viability and of social impact of PPP projects; (b) PPP contracts themselves are not made public; (c) budget documentation does not include disclosures of rights, obligations, and other exposures under PPP contracts; and (d) PPP liabilities are not explicitly included in debt statistics, budget documentation, and fiscal reports, and contingent PPP liabilities are also not disclosed in budget documents or fiscal risk reports/statements.

[84] See, for example, Bhatta and Huseynov, 2024, for a study on technical and vocational education and training in Azerbaijan.
[85] Government of Turkmenistan. 2023. *Voluntary National Review of Turkmenistan*. Ashgabat, pp. 31 and 157.
[86] IMF. 2020. *Republic of Kazakhstan, Selected Issues. Country* Report No. 20/38. Washington, DC, p. 55.

Table 7. Institutional Overload for Public–Private Partnerships in Kazakhstan

	Entity	Role
1	Cabinet	Approves the list of "PPP projects of special importance" and the list of PPP facilities that require a closed competitive bidding process
2	Ministry of National Economy	Oversees the state policy and framework for implementing PPP projects as well as coordination of PPP activities; also provides the regulations for setting limits of total concession/PPP obligations at the republican and local levels)
3	State Budget Commission	Approves limits on concession/PPP commitments
4	Ministry of Finance	Registers all PPP contracts, checks that liabilities associated with future payments do not go beyond set limits, and executes state guarantee agreements and state surety agreements
5	Line ministries	Manage PPP projects within their sectors, prepare concession proposals, and organize tenders or direct negotiations
6	*Akimats* (subnational executive bodies)	Oversee smaller-scale regional PPP projects, prepare project proposals, and act as organizers of tender processes or direct negotiations (with the assistance of regional PPP centers)
7	PPP Center JSC (fully owned by government agency)	Provides due diligence and advisory services to the Government, and monitors concession/PPP projects on behalf of the Government; mainly provides support during tenders, assists with the coordination of project monitoring, keeps the PPP project register, and renders methodological advice and training to regional PPP centers
8	Kazyna Capital Management JSC (affiliate of Baiterek NMH Joint Stock Company)	Assists with PPP project development at the national level in these functions: a. Developing pre-project documentation with the assistance of qualified consultants (business plans, draft PPP contracts, etc.) b. Advising PPP projects in obtaining approvals and expert conclusions of relevant government entities c. Attracting local and international investors and institutions with the application of the Holding's tools and its broad international network d. Advising during negotiations between the parties of PPP contracts
9	*Atameken* (Chamber of Entrepreneurs)	Participates in tender commissions and in monitoring the implementation of signed PPP projects

PPP = public–private partnership.
Source: ADB country diagnostic work for CPS for Kazakhstan, 2022, citing ADB. 2019a. *Public–Private Partnership Monitor*, 2nd Edition. Manila. pp. 318–319.

Some other challenges that can be documented when it comes to PPPs are as follows:

(a) Non-transparent investment incentives framework, as evident by, for example, no formal set of criteria in place to determine which exemptions and incentives apply to a particular project. This then implies that investment incentives are negotiated on a case-by-case basis. From a transparency perspective, when the exemptions and incentives that are granted thus to projects are not made public, it is difficult to claim there has been credible commitment demonstrated by the government towards an effective PPP architecture.

(b) This element of non-transparency also generally extends to areas such as concession applications and decisions as well as feasibility studies and environmental and social impact assessments.

(c) If the legal arrangements do not necessarily mandate competitive bidding (or that bid results must be made public), then PPP projects can (arguably) be awarded on a negotiated basis. This negates efforts to foster a more welcoming PPP environment in which the private sector has confidence.

(d) Governments do not normally shy away from using tools such as the Swiss Challenge in PPPs,[87] on which there are not generally any issues. It is when governments misuse the tool (such as automatically shortlisting private investors submitting an unsolicited proposal, even when they do not offer the lowest price) that trust in the system is compromised.

(e) A common constraint evident in DMCs is gaps across the board on capacity and resources to roll out, and effectively implement, the government's PPP agenda. This capacity gap is with respect to knowledge of, and experiences in, PPP projects among public sector staff.

(f) The World Bank's 2021 assessment[88] of the PPP situation in Lao PDR concluded that the opportunistic nature of unsolicited proposals combined with an absence of competitive tendering and the government's limited capacity to effectively negotiate contracts has adversely impacted the value-for-money from PPP projects and contributed to increasing direct and contingent liabilities for the government.

The last point on governments not uniformly and rigorously assessing fiscal risks and contingent liabilities associated with PPPs prior to approval of new projects is critical and relates to the issues already discussed in the previous section. IMF's 2018 PIMA for Viet Nam noted that the preparation, appraisal, selection, and monitoring processes for PPP projects were incomplete, which exposed the government to significant fiscal risks.[89] It recommended to enhance the capacity of the MOF and others to analyze and manage fiscal risks associated with PPP projects, including by introducing a clearer "gateway process" for selecting PPP projects and by reinforcing monitoring of contingent liabilities.

Other Considerations on PSD

On procurement. Given the importance of the public procurement function in the economy, it is useful to see the role of the private sector in procurement processes across DMCs. In Fiji, for example, there is a reasonably developed private sector that responds to the procurement needs of the government, while large-value contracts attract international response. The private sector in Fiji is also increasingly receptive to sustainable procurement (SusPP) requirements. Mongolia's Vision 2050 has set SusPP targets with a share of green public procurement in total government procurement of 10% in 2025, 20% in 2030, and 50% in 2050, the more interesting feature being the objective to gradually shift public procurement to green procurement and create a private sector support system by 2030.

One of the critical elements of the Philippine government's transformation agenda includes partnership with the private sector.[90] This is evident in the composition and work of the Government Procurement Policy Board–a statutory, independent, and interagency body responsible for the regulatory function in public procurement, whose membership includes representatives from various government departments and a private sector representative.

With respect to SOEs. In many countries, government support to SOEs has meant the private sector does not find it as easy to enter the market. As far as market access is concerned, most of the problems germinate from the range of subsidies given to SOEs to enter into, and flourish in, the market. According to private firms, they are disadvantaged in competing against SOEs for government-financed contracts due to the SOEs' conflicts of interest, historical relationships with procuring units, and advantages in obtaining preferential access to capital, land, and resources. Despite the sale of government shareholdings in SOEs, ministries in many cases retain a substantial share.

87 The "Swiss challenge" is a bidding process used in PPPs where a government agency allows other companies to propose improvements to an unsolicited project proposal from an original party. If a better proposal is submitted, the original party gets a chance to match it; if it does not, the project goes to the best competing bidder.

88 World Bank. 2021. *PPP Legal, Regulatory and Institutional Framework Gap Analysis in Lao PDR.* Vientiane. p. 48.

89 The government only had a partial view of contingent liabilities arising from PPP projects at local and central levels since there was no formal requirement for reporting contingent liabilities arising from PPPs; International Monetary Fund. 2018. *Vietnam, Public Investment Management Assessment – PIMA.* Washington, DC. p. 8.

90 The others are: (a) digitalization; (b) servicification to foster intersectoral linkages; (c) dynamic innovation ecosystem; (d) enhanced connectivity; (e) greater collaboration between local and national government; and (f) ensuring sound fiscal management and improving the tax regime.

On access to information. For the private sector to be an equal partner in the economy, it is required that the sector has access to information for more effective and efficient decision-making. But, clearly, this is not the case in many instances. The absence of information constrains the decision-making space for the private sector, and the scope to adequately consider risks to enter markets is severely constrained for the firms.

On gender equality. Increasingly, and from an intersectional perspective, efforts to enhance PSD are also directed at issues of gender equality and women's empowerment. ADB's work with DMC clients to advance gender equality by integrating actions that empower women and narrow gender gaps is noteworthy. This integration is both in the design and implementation of projects.

ADB's focus on gender equality in private sector operations is based on five pillars: (a) economic empowerment of women through skills building and greater financial inclusion; (b) investments in educational and health projects that narrow gender gaps; (c) enhancing gender equality in decision-making and leadership through, for example, corporate-sponsored mentorship programs for aspiring women leaders; (d) reducing women's time poverty through investments that utilize appropriate technologies; and (e) strengthening women's resilience to climate change, ensuring gender-responsive, and post-conflict reconstruction efforts (see **Box 16** for a brief description of ADB's initiative called Women's Finance Exchange).

Box 16. ADB's Women's Finance Exchange Program

The Program's focus on: (a) building capacity by offering tailored support to financial institutions to enhance their capacity to deliver financial services for women entrepreneurs; (b) finding funding (and co-financing) opportunities to boost lending to women and women's businesses; (c) identifying technology solutions as part of the support to financial institutions for gender-responsive and sustainable financing; and (d) supporting sustainability by helping financial institutions in "greening" their portfolios.

The Program is active in all the DMCs, although current engagement in terms of specific projects are in countries such as Papua New Guinea, Fiji, Georgia, the Lao People's Democratic Republic, Nepal, Viet Nam, and elsewhere.

Source: https://www.wfx.adb.org/ (accessed 4 February 2026).

On other areas. At a broad level, the Philippine government after COVID-19 identified priority structural reforms under the economic resiliency plan, Plan for a Healthy and Resilient Philippines in which the private sector has been given due importance. For example, the plan calls for strong measures in (a) digitalization / streamlining of transactions with government and private sector; (b) investments—economic liberalization bills, modernization of investment promotion agencies; and (c) businesses—ease of credit, regulatory reforms to improve competition, foster innovation, and digitalization.

The key strands of work on the part of governments to determine the scope and scale of PSD in a country is encompassed in market creation, opportunities matching, and promotion of investment opportunities. All of these are also inherent in the establishment of a favorable macro environment for PSD.

Some Key Issues to Note on PSD

Productive consultations. Establishing transparent consultation mechanisms is of strategic importance for any government seeking to foster economic growth. These mechanisms are the foundation upon which trust is built, policy effectiveness is ensured, and a stable and predictable environment for private investment is created. When the private sector has clear, fair, and accessible channels for communication and grievance, it is more likely to invest with confidence and partner with the government on national priorities. The role of independent commissions can ensure fairness and accountability as they play critical roles in acting as impartial arbiters between public and private interest.

Investment-friendly policies. There is great emphasis on the importance of proactive government measures to incentivize private sector investments. The Kyrgyz Republic offers compelling examples of initiatives to actively improve the operating climate for private enterprise.

(a) **PPP Center:** With support from ADB, the government established a PPP Center to coordinate project implementation and provide technical support. This has successfully catalyzed new projects in key sectors like transport and energy, creating structured opportunities for private investment in national infrastructure.
(b) **Digitalization and de-bureaucratization:** The government is pursuing initiatives to reduce direct interactions between business owners and government officials. This is particularly valuable as it serves to build confidence by making processes more transparent and less prone to transactional friction.
(c) **Strengthening rule of law:** A focused effort to enforce laws and reduce criminality has directly improved the overall investment environment, signaling a commitment to security and stability that is crucial for attracting and retaining private capital.

A cross-cutting issue: primacy of strong institutions. In country contexts where political and economic stability is not robust and cannot be assumed outright, strong oversight institutions are seen as the ultimate safeguard for investors. The ability to weather political transitions depends on having independent institutions that have the fundamental systems in place. The patronage networks evident in many developing countries are a direct consequence of a lack of the very institutional independence championed in others elsewhere. The absence of impartial and empowered bodies allows such an extractive model to flourish, where political connections supersede market principles. Strong institutions thus provide the predictability and rule of law that are the true bedrock of a stable and attractive investment climate.

A collaborative framework for advancing the national development agenda. Governments need to consider a strategic shift in thinking beyond simply creating a favorable business climate. The emerging consensus is that true partnership involves actively aligning private sector capabilities with national development goals. This approach moves from a passive, regulatory relationship to an active, collaborative one where private enterprise becomes an engine for achieving specific social and developmental outcomes, such as gender equality, environmental protection, and human capital development.

PSD as a result of a strong public sector. Finally, development of the private sector in the DMCs is closely associated with the strength of the public sector. Reliance on the work of strengthened PSM resulting from ADB's sovereign operations means that PSD will continue to be a function of a strong public sector. Thus, issues such as robust macrofiscal environments, tax transparency and simplicity, good corporate governance, strong government support for technical and vocational education and training, clear and transparent public procurement processes, strong anticorruption measures, and simple business registration and management requirements will directly influence the scale of PSD at country levels.

Maximizing Digitalization for Effective Service Delivery

Introduction

Digitalization – and ICT, in general – is an important theme for purposes of enhancement of governance. It not only enables better service delivery to recipients but also helps the government to minimize any situation of information asymmetry in the system. It intrinsically prompts the government to target specific areas of improvement based on real-time feedback as decision-makers are able to better manage government operations. That digitalization also helps improve transparency adds to the need to robustly champion its role in governance reforms.

However, although basic coverage of the population by a mobile network across the DMCs in the region is not dire, not all countries have advanced systems. ADB's database for 2024[91] shows DMCs such as Georgia, Maldives, Mongolia, Viet Nam, Azerbaijan, and many others with 100% (or close to it) of their population covered by a mobile network. Indeed, smartphone adoption in Asia and the Pacific is expected to go up from 78% in 2022 to 94% by 2030, above the global average of 92%.

Digitalization in National Policies

In many DMCs, the impetus for digitalization in the economy has been grounded at the level of national policy and strategy themselves. In the Kyrgyz Republic, for instance, the 2018–2040 National Development Strategy declares that official economic policy will be focused on reforms to create a competitive digital economy by attracting entrepreneurs and applying innovative and environmentally friendly technologies.

In Viet Nam, the Socio-Economic Development Strategy 2021–2030 has outlined several ambitious reform agendas, one of which is to place strong emphasis on digital transformation as a cross-cutting driver in order to renew its growth model and enhance its competitiveness. The government in July 2021 approved the State Administration Reform Master Plan 2021–2030, which focuses on six areas, one of which is development of e-government and digital government.

For the Philippines, the overarching goal of the Philippine Development Plan 2023–2028, is deep economic and social transformation to reinvigorate job creation and accelerate poverty reduction.[92] The plan aims to achieve upper middle-income country status by 2025. One of the key elements of the transformation agenda includes digitalization.

With particular reference to service delivery enhancements, the discussion on digitalization can be seen from a broader perspective. This is evident in, for example, the Digital Indonesia Vision 2045. The focus of the Vision is on three end-state attributes: (a) *inclusive*: equitable availability of digital access and safe digital space for all levels of society; (b) *empowering*: the ability of the community to utilize digital technology productively and create added value from its utilization; and (c) *sustainable*: digital transformation is based on fulfilling the SDGs.

The Digital Indonesia Vision 2045 espouses the following inter-related goals which can be seen as being sequential in **Figure 9**.

Implications of Digitalization vis-à-vis Governance

Digitalization is increasingly seen as an essential component of good governance. Its implications on elements of governments can be seen from various angles. For example, institutional structures (at all levels of government) are critical if digitalization services are to be effectively provided. In Nepal, the government's promotion of digitalization in the public sphere is reflected in the work of the E-Governance Commission, which is making a significant effort to ensure seamless delivery of services online by all levels of government, including constitutional bodies. Towards this end, the Commission is working on a Digital Nepal Blueprint.

DMCs are also increasingly focusing on creating the right conditions to stimulate investments in national *digital infrastructure*. The costs of such investments are high, for which there is increasing consideration given to bringing in the private sector in this area. Also, understanding that technology cannot be sector- or space-focused, DMCs' e-government strategy has tended to be that implementation of the relevant policies not only be limited to governments (including the central, provincial [regional] and local bodies) but also incorporate the private sector.

91 ADB. 2024b. 2024 Basic Statistics (accessed 18 August 2025).

92 National Economic and Development Authority. 2023. *Philippine Development Plan 2023–2028*.

Figure 9. Goals of Digital Indonesia Vision 2045

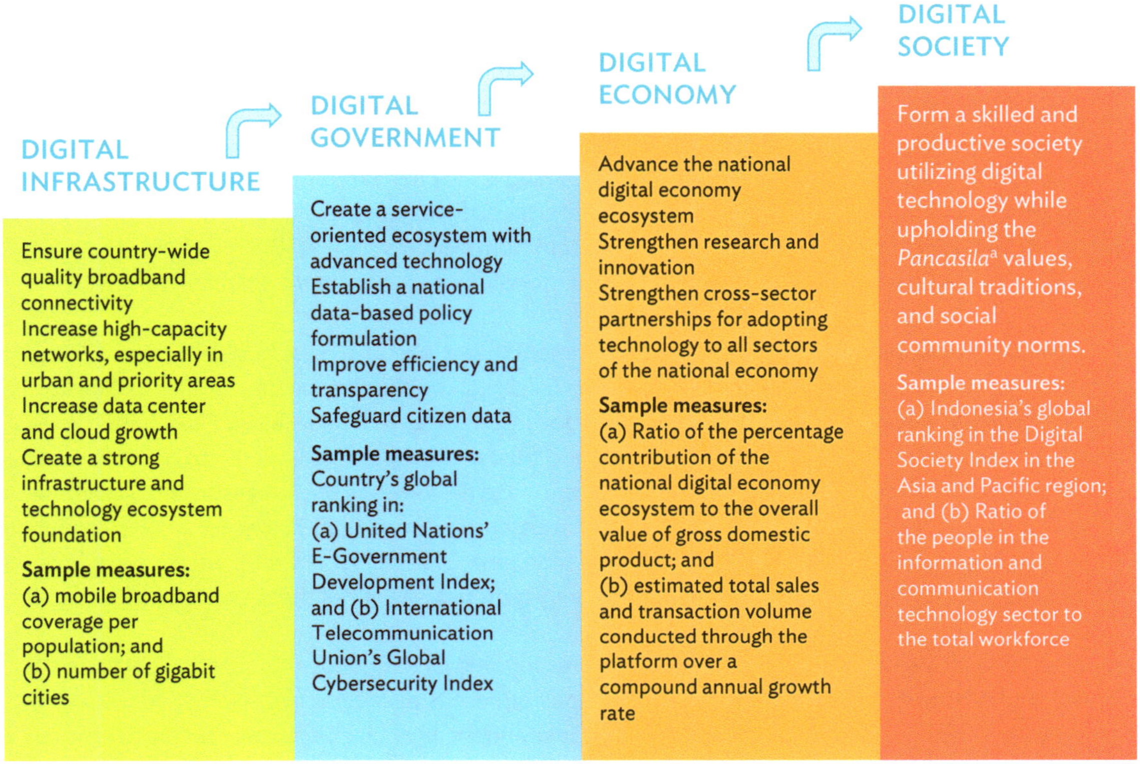

Note:

[a] *Pancasila* values: the five principles of Indonesian society are: (a) belief in the one and only God; (b) just and civilized humanity; (c) unity of Indonesia; (d) democracy, led by the wisdom of the representatives of the people; and (e) social justice for all Indonesian people.

Source: Ministry of Communication and Informatics. 2023. Digital Indonesia: Vision 2045. Jakarta; and https://www.kemhan.go.id/wp-content/uploads/2017/11/wiraenglishweb.pdf (accessed 20 August 2025).

On the other hand, digitalization and electronic data exchange among government agencies are often affected by outdated and duplicated licensing services, inadequate technical capacities, varying standards, and uneven levels of readiness. For example, in Mongolia, some agencies have created their own e-service systems that are not compatible with the E-Mongolia platform, and there have been instances of lack of collaboration among government agencies in terms of their digitalization work.

On governance-related systems, the focus has largely centered on the application of technology in *improving the public procurement systems* and processes (particularly on e-GP). Attention here has been on improving the functionality and security of the government e-procurement system by developing and introducing data asymmetric encryption and digital signature and procurement and installation of equipment critical for data management. Across the DMCs, the intent is to fully digitalize the e-procurement system and help shift all government procurement transactions online with better functionality and security.

The use of technology to *improve the national tax system* is also something that is evident in all DMCs. This has several dimensions: not only is the focus on making it easier for tax filers (individuals as well as enterprises) to pay their taxes (thus facilitating greater coverage), but also to improve the efficiency of such collection (thus reducing transaction costs to governments). Various tax administration diagnostic assessment exercises that have been carried out across DMCs shows that one of the significant strengths of national tax agencies (such as the Bureau of Internal Revenue in the Philippines or the Mongolian Tax Authority) is their ability to leverage technology as the key driver to implement several initiatives to improve tax administration and enhance services to citizens.

On *accountability*, the applications of technology in government actions are clear to see. One particular emphasis here is on the augmentation of accountability in the governance system through the use of technology. SAIs in select DMCs (such as the Office of the Comptroller and Auditor General in Bangladesh) have effectively begun to put these into practice. However, despite such benefits, the Office has faced several challenges that hinder its effectiveness. These include limited access to financial data from systems such as iBAS++ and Automated System for Customs Data, and insufficient integration of e-audit modules into government digital platforms.

To ensure greater *social and gender inclusiveness*, governments have begun to create online portals that create a community where knowledge can be shared, and which offer digital tools and resources for the marginalized groups to gain better access to services. Not having to physically be present to receive social welfare funds for those infirm or with disabilities, for example, enhances service delivery and trust in the system as well. It also helps governments to build institutions in identifying digital solutions that can respond to the needs of the female business segment. Access for marginalized groups and remote areas, however, is a substantive concern. In Nepal, for example, while mobile penetration is at approximately 130% of the total population, only 37% of Nepalis have access to mobile Internet services with a substantial number of people in rural and very remote areas out of the access picture altogether.

On empowerment. Picking up on the previous point on responding to the needs of the female business segment, the implications to how digitalization can enhance empowerment is also clear. Technology has enabled greater financial inclusion and scope for individuals to make independent financial decisions (such as for rural women to carry out small financial transactions independently). This is not a trivial impact of technology in the broader development objectives of gender empowerment.

The discussions above point to the various implications of digitalization on governance, including PFM and other processes, as enumerated in **Box 17**.

Constraints to Digitalization

There are inherent as well as emerging constraints to effective digitalization; for example:

(a) Lack of clear and up-to-date policies that specifically address the unique requirements of digitalization in all aspects of the economy and socio-political domains.
(b) Insufficient intellectual property protection, and inadequate regulations for data privacy and security (the dearth of cybersecurity laws and of support for data security are issues that have been mentioned often in government policy circles).
(c) Limited service coverage, particularly for marginalized groups and those in remote areas of countries.[93]
(d) Many government agencies have developed independent siloed systems over time (e.g., for debt management). These legacy systems often do not easily communicate with one another, preventing a unified view of public finances and hindering a whole-of-government approach.
(e) Sub-optimal collaboration among public sector agencies entrusted with managing this sector. Such collaboration among different stakeholders (e.g., on PPPs, and university-industry collaboration) is necessary for driving rapid digital transformation and embedding the right practices and processes in the system itself.

93 Indeed, a serious lack of digital infrastructure is the reason for expensive internet services; see Deloitte Consulting, 2022 for a case on Nepal (*Nepal Digital Services Sector: Market Systems Assessment.* USAID Trade and Competitiveness Activity. Kathmandu).

Box 17. Public Sector Management and Digitalization

Domain	Specific Public Sector Management (PSM) Action
Public investments	Needed to enhance digital access to remote and lagging regions; develop a nation-wide broadband backbone; put in place basic infrastructure for electricity supply and transport
Regulation	In order to ensure affordable quality services, there is need for appropriate regulation
Privacy	Governments need to ensure adequate protection of personal data and privacy; given existing vulnerabilities in the selected developing member countries, this is a critical PSM action to be taken
Access vs. content	There is a need to balance the focus of government action between providing access to digital technology and helping develop more useful and directly relevant content that will aid targeted service delivery to where it is needed
Intellectual property rights	Governments are increasingly asked to ensure that these rights are safeguarded through effective regulations and enforcement of the same
Access to data/information	Concurrently, governments need to ensure that citizens have ready and adequate access to information and data at affordable costs; the "last mile" connectivity support is also crucial
Competition	Competition policy is always important, and as large technology firms begin to enter the market, there is more compelling need for the competition policy to be strengthened and applied fairly
Legal arrangements against crime	Cases of cybercrime (including financial in nature), hacking, etc. are on the rise, and it is incumbent on governments to ensure that there are legal and other relevant and suitable arrangements in place in the PSM domain to effectively address them

Source: Bhatta, 2020, Table 11.1, page 211 ('Those that fix the lights'...: The Practice of Public Sector Management in Developing Asia, 1st ed., by Gambhir Bhatta, Copyright (2020) by Routledge. Reproduced by permission of Taylor & Francis Group).

Also seen as a constraint, and meriting greater attention across DMCs, is inadequate capability and coordination among the agencies to embrace an ecosystem for digital governance and advancing effective digitalization at both central and SNG levels with tangible impact of digitalization on effective service delivery. This requires effective on-boarding of all the stakeholders for long-term digitalization for which, in turn, identifying (and continuously engaging with) some early champions in key entities in government is critical.

Constraints on digitalization have also been evident as a result of outdated and duplicated licensing services, inadequate technical capacities, varying standards, and uneven levels of readiness, as in the E-Mongolia platform.[94] There, some agencies have created their own e-service system which are not compatible with the E-Mongolia platform.

Some Key Issues to Note on Digitalization

On Service Delivery. A particular issue on the subject of digitalization has increasingly been centered on that of service delivery. This aspect (through the use of technology) has been extended to constitute a third form of decentralization, termed 'virtual decentralization'. Indeed, analysis carried out by, for example, Goel and Saunois (2017) shows that not only is virtual decentralization "more effective in controlling both corruption and the shadow economy," but that it is also cheaper, faster, with greater spatial reach, and with less potential for bureaucracy (i.e., red tape). [1] Programs in countries such as Bangladesh and Bhutan, for instance, have been predicated on these assumptions and revealed experiences.[95]

[94] UNESCAP. 2019. Readiness Assessment for Cross-border Paperless Trade: Mongolia (accessed 27 January 2026).

[95] Footnote 31, p. 3.

Indeed, analysis carried out by, for example, Goel and Saunois (2017) shows that not only is virtual decentralization "more effective in controlling both corruption and the shadow economy," but that it is also cheaper, faster, with greater spatial reach, and with less potential for bureaucracy (i.e., red tape).[96] Programs in Bangladesh, Bhutan, and elsewhere, for instance, have been predicated on these assumptions and revealed experiences.

Digitalization and information asymmetry. Digitalization is an important theme for purposes of enhancement of governance in a country not only because it enables better service delivery to recipients, but also because it enables the government to minimize any situation of information asymmetry in the system. It prompts the government to target specific areas of improvement based on real-time feedback.

Digitalization of governance and the development of digital infrastructure in the selected DMCs has also been evident in how technology can directly contribute to better service delivery on the ground.[97] Access to such technology is important here although it has been clear that across many DMCs the focus is still on the access and the infrastructure, rather than the content. One particular element of the focus on digitalization and service delivery improvements has also been on seeking to systematically connect businesses to the electronic government system. Also, service delivery improvements through one-stop digital portals, such as the *Nagarik Sewa Kendra* (citizen services center) in Nepal, are gaining greater currency.

Accessing public services and information is not always necessarily simple. Individuals and businesses may have to submit a variety of applications through multiple channels, both on paper and electronically, and they may submit the same information more than once because of the lack of a centralized database. Further, some services, such as the courts or certain audits, require hard copies of documentation. Accessibility could be improved by integrating the various agencies' systems, having a centralized database, and/or putting in place an effective information exchange system.

Enabling environment for digitalization. All governments are now fully on board that digital acceleration will be at the forefront of how they provide services to citizens, as well as with how digitalization will impact the nature and composition of the national workforce, and how digitally enabled environments will dictate all facets of national life. The overarching risk here is that government policymakers and regulators may not be able to create an enabling environment where digitalization will be the force multiplier for more effective service delivery.[98] There is a fair bit of policy dialogue and debate on this last issue, particularly on just how well the governments can balance their roles as enablers and as regulators.

Technology fallacy. Technology and digitalization are a gamechanger in all spheres of the economy and social affairs. Indeed, the rapid development of digital technology is seen as the most significant driver of innovation and competition that will propel national economies. Still, governments need to be aware of the "Technology Fallacy," that is, the common misconception that technology is a complete solution in itself. Technology is merely an enabler. This fact requires governments to work towards a strategic shift in approach. The most effective strategy is to rethink and re-engineer processes and procedures *before* applying technology. Developing multiple, uncoordinated systems, even with good aims, leads to inefficiency.

96 R. Goel and J. Saunois. 2017. Forms of Government Decentralization and Institutional Quality: Evidence from a Large Sample of Nations. In N. Yoshino, and P. Morgan (eds.), *Central and Local Government Relations in Asia: Achieving Fiscal Sustainability*. Cheltenham, UK, and Northampton, US: Edward Elgar Publishing. pp. 395–419.

97 For a cogent analysis of the link between digitalization and service delivery, see ADB. 2025c (Chapter 5).

98 See, for example, S. Bhatnagar. 2015. Using ICT to Improve Governance and Service Delivery to the Poor. In B. Deolalikar, S. Jha, and P. Quising (eds.), *Governance in Developing Asia: Public Service Delivery and Empowerment*. ADB, and Edgar Elgar Publishing, Cheltenham, UK. pp. 296–322.

Focusing on Climate and Disaster Resilience

Introduction

Four of the DMCs covered in this study (the atoll nations of Kiribati, Maldives, RMI, and Tuvalu) have been described as facing an existential threat from rising seas and shrinking natural resources; in short, among the most vulnerable to the profound impacts of climate change. This drives home the importance of managing the adverse effects of climate change through updated and enhanced policies, laws, and institutions.

ADB notes that without adaptation, impacts of climate risks could increase the economic damage from coastal flooding in atoll nations by nearly 200 times by the end of the century under high-emission scenarios.[99] This would result in economic damages ranging from 18% to 58% of their GDPs, leading to a clearly unsustainable financial situation for these countries. There are other adverse impacts as well, including that of salinization of vulnerable freshwater sources in these countries. The experiences of countries such as the four mentioned here, and indeed of many other DMCs, in similar predicaments – bolstered by analytical work of ADB and others – infer clearly a strong focus on resilience broadly defined.[100]

On Climate Change

All DMCs face increasing environmental pressures from climate change. These pressures have always clearly implied how they course into those related to financing needs in order to mitigate, and adapt to, the effects of climate change. The 2021 Climate Policy Initiative, for example, stated that, to avoid the most dangerous impacts of climate change, global climate financial flows need to be accelerated (an increase of at least 590% in annual climate finance is needed to meet the target of keeping global warming within a 1.5°C scenario by 2030).[101]

DMCs are also uniformly susceptible to the adverse impacts of climate change. For example, Nepal, which ranked fourth in the world in terms of climate change susceptibility,[102] has had to face hurdles in putting in place measures that will help it deal with climate change issues. Further, gaps in financing are not the only issues; institutional gaps, lack of awareness and often of political commitment as well on needed climate action, are also evident.

In many countries, functions related to climate action are largely centralized and the integration of the central government budget with climate strategies and actions is still work in progress. To build an effective country platform to respond to the ambitious climate targets, specific roles and mandates need to be established, particularly for the SNGs (as well as for other important actors, such as the private sector and civil society).

This focus on SNGs in the domain of climate change and disaster resilience has taken on an even more critical dimension in countries where political and institutional maturity on subnational governance is still evolving. In Nepal, for example, even though the Environmental Protection Act 2019 has provisions for SNG roles in climate action, there are no clear and defined roles and responsibilities for them to meet the national climate targets. This, in turn, affects the level of accountability in climate budget management and reporting.

---

99 ADB. 2022b. *Sea-Level Change in the Pacific Islands Region: A Review of Evidence to Inform Asian Development Bank Guidance on Selecting Sea-Level Projections for Climate Risk and Adaptation Assessments*. Manila.

100 The general meaning of "resilience" (i.e., of successfully coping with, in the short term; and managing, in the long term) of any adverse situation signifies the ability of societies and governments to bounce back from adversity. In terms of climate change impacts this would be, for example, managing the realities of a warmer world.

101 Asian Development Bank. 2023b. *Climate Finance Landscape of Asia and the Pacific*. Manila.

102 Center for Social Change. 2023. Disaster Risk Governance (accessed 22 August 2025).

On Disaster Resilience

All DMCs are susceptible to disasters, some more than others. Mongolia, for example, is deemed to be one of the most disaster-prone countries in the world because it is susceptible to *dzuds* (severe winter colds and/or heavy snow associated with large-scale livestock losses), dust storms, droughts, floods, wildfires, and earthquakes. It is extremely vulnerable to natural hazards because of its geographical location, and continental climate that directly influences the nature, scale, and frequency of hazards experienced.[103] Indeed, it has been reported that, on average, from 2001 to 2021, the economic loss caused by natural and human-induced hazards in Mongolia amounted to $28.4 million per year (or 2% of the country's GDP).[104]

As the COVID-19 pandemic demonstrated, it is not only natural hazards that DMCs need to be mindful of. Quite apart from the substantial loss of life, and long-term effects of ill-health, there were also pressures imposed on the fiscal capacities of governments to respond and to sustain the livelihoods of millions of people who relied on the government safety net. Coupled with large drawdowns on financial reserves as well as a loss in resource mobilization, the pandemic drove home the need for governments to be prepared for such disasters in the future. In particular, this has meant putting in place robust fiscal policies and measures and strengthening their PFM systems as well.

Review of efforts to enhance disaster resilience shows that proper action is centered on: (a) robust policy, institutional, and regulatory measures; (b) disaster risk financing, including from leveraging private sector investments; (c) specific disaster-prevention measures (such as early warning systems, flood control); and (d) community preparedness. It has become clear now that investments in these areas have the most far-reaching effect if they are carefully integrated into the development process.

Climate and Disaster Resilience and Public Financial Management

On both climate change and disaster resilience (or the cumulative term used here: climate and disaster resilience [CDR]) as they relate to macrofiscal and governance considerations, key issues are: (a) resource requirements, and project/program design and development to adapt and mitigate the adverse impacts of CDR; (b) governance arrangements that need to be in place in order to ensure that governments have a good handle on CDR issues as they impact the achievement of development goals (including the SDGs); and (c) associated issues of fiscal risks that necessarily emerge in this discussion of CDR policies.

CDR can be systematically embedded across the entire PFM cycle through concrete actions as shown in **Table 8**.

On *resource requirements and program design*, the focus is on incentivizing investments by the private sector as well since public resource envelopes are not substantial enough to cater to the full needs. Leveraging other resourcing provisions, such as green local currency-denominated bonds for infrastructure development, financing facilities for green infrastructure, and guarantees for renewable energy and energy storage projects are also relevant here.

Governance arrangements on CDR normally center on legal, policy, regulatory, and institutional arrangements to best address relevant issues. And all pertinent elements of PFM (such as budgeting, legislative scrutiny, procurement, tax administration, fiscal decentralization, etc.) are also valid.

103 Asian Development Bank. 2019b. *Mongolia: Strengthening Capacity on Disaster Risk Assessment, Reduction, and Transfer Instruments in Mongolia.* Manila.

104 B. Ariuntungalag. 2022. Country Report: Mongolia. Asian Disaster Reduction Center.

Table 8. Climate and Disaster Resilience and Public Financial Management

PFM Stage	Practical Measures
Planning	• **Mainstream plans:** Integrate costed climate and disaster plans into National Development Plans to ensure they are resourced. • **Fiscal risk statements:** Quantify and include climate and disaster risks in these statements.
Budgeting	• **Signal priorities:** Include climate resilience as a priority in budget call circulars. • **Mandate assessments:** Require climate and disaster risk assessments for all new budget measures. • **Budget for financing instruments:** Allocate funds for insurance premiums, or disaster funds.
Budget Execution	• **Emergency procurement:** Establish transparent and rapid emergency procurement protocols to be activated during a disaster. • **Green procurement:** Leverage the government's purchasing power to promote sustainable goods and services.
Accounting & Reporting	• **Budget tagging:** Use climate and disaster budget tagging to track expenditures and ensure funds are used effectively. • **Expenditure reviews:** Conduct public expenditure reviews to prevent leakages in disaster fund spending. • **Track Nationally Determined Contributions:** Monitor the implementation and effectiveness of these contributions.

GDP = gross domestic product, PFM = public financial management.
Source: Authors, based on a review of various ADB reports.

On climate-related PFM and risks. Effectively addressing CDR issues inherently incur substantial fiscal as well as other risks. As such, issues of risk financing and risk transfer mechanisms, as well as risks inherent in the broader PFM sphere, with respect to CDR are also relevant. One particular tool being increasingly used to assess the degree of fiscal risks resulting from non-adherence to robust climate action by governments is the climate-responsive component of the PEFA assessment. Since PEFA results are used extensively to ascertain risks in other parts of the macrofiscal environment, the tool also provides complementary scope to look at fiscal risks resulting from climate inaction by governments.

Another useful assessment tool for gauging disaster resilience of a country's PFM systems is the World Bank's Disaster Resilient and Responsive Public Financial Management.[105] The Philippines undertook this assessment in 2025, with ADB support, to determine the extent to which disaster resilience and responsiveness are embedded in its PFM systems. **Figure 10** shows the integration of disaster resilience and responsiveness into 27 PFM elements in the Philippines.

Table 9 presents the summary results of climate-related PEFA assessments carried out in the DMCs covered in this study, and for which the results are in the public domain: Bhutan (2023), Indonesia (2022), Nepal (2024), and Samoa (2021).

Good practices. Even as the overall assessment scores for the four DMCs on climate PEFA are not as robust as one would expect, there are still practices that other DMCs could consider applying to their own context. As such, few as they are, all A scores are highlighted here for the DMCs as well as the practice notes as documented by the assessors (**Table 10**).

105 World Bank. 2022. *Disaster Resilient and Responsive Public Financial Management: An Assessment Tool*. Washington, DC.

Figure 10. Integration of Disaster Resilience and Responsiveness into Public Financial Management Elements
(Philippines)

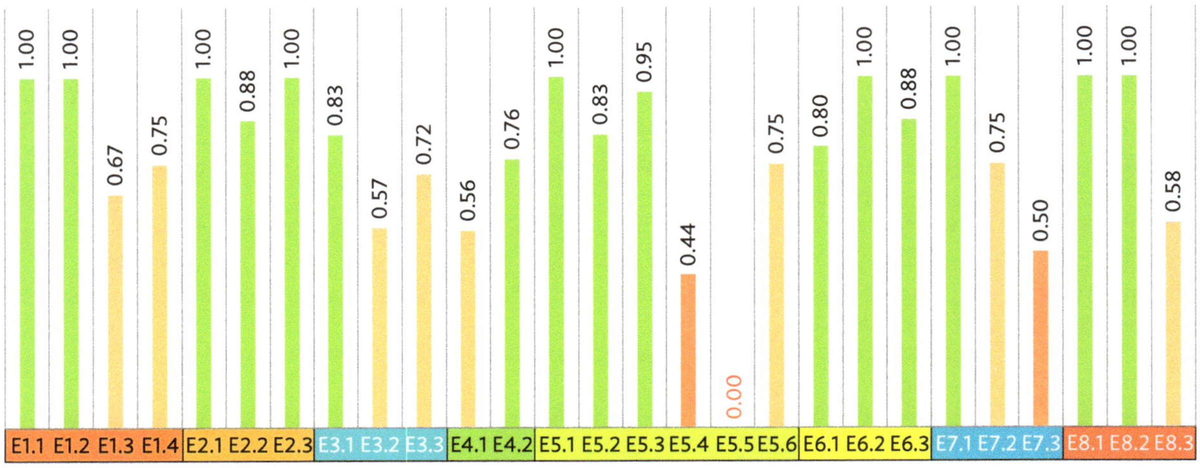

CFA = Central Finance Agency, DRM = domestic resource mobilization, DRR = disaster resilience and responsiveness, PFM = public financial management.

Notes:

1. Pillar 1: DRR-PFM Institutional Arrangements; E1.1: Disaster proclamation; E1.2: Institutional mandate for disaster risk management; E1.3: CFA capacity for DRM; E1.4: CFA business continuity planning.
2. Pillar 2: Resilient Information Systems and Records; E2.1: Regulatory framework; E2.2: Planning for Information Technology resilience; E2.3: Information Technology resilience.
3. Pillar 3: Planning and Budgeting for DRM; E3.1: Fiscal risk assessment; E3.2: Expenditure planning for disaster risk reduction and resilience; E3.3: Financing of disaster response and recovery.
4. Pillar 4: Disaster- Informed Public Investment and Asset Management; E4.1: Disaster-informed public investment management; E4.2: Disaster-informed asset management.
5. Pillar 5: Budget Management, Control, and Reporting during Disasters; E5.1: Post-disaster treasury management; E5.2: Post-disaster budget flexibility; E5.3: Post-disaster expenditure control; E5.4: Accounting for and tracking disaster-related expenditure; E5.5: Post-disaster internal audit; E5.6: Transparency of disaster-related expenditure.
6. Pillar 6: Disaster- Responsive Public Procurement; E6.1: Procurement planning for post-disaster response; E6.2: Expedited procurement procedures; E6.3: Contract management.
7. Pillar 7: Disaster- Responsive Audit and Oversight; E7.1: External Audit; E7.2: Legislative Oversight; E7.3: Participation.
8. Pillar 8: Social Inclusion; E8.1: Policy Framework and Planning for Social Inclusion; E8.2: Institutional Coordination for Social Inclusion in disaster risk management; E8.3: Social Inclusion-Informed Budget System for DRM.
9. Scores are between 0 [Lowest] to 1 [Highest]. The color of the bar graphs denotes degree of integration of disaster risk.

Source: Republic of the Philippines. 2025. *Philippines Disaster Resilient and Responsive-Public Financial Management (DRR-PFM) Assessment Report*.

Some of the more relevant B scores for the DMCs also merit mention here:

(a) On ***climate-related debt and guarantees***. In Bhutan, the purposes for which the government may borrow are specified in the legal framework and include climate-related liabilities; the MOF may on-lend to public corporations and local governments. In Indonesia, the legal framework that allows the government to borrow also covers climate-related liabilities. The regulatory framework also allows SNGs and public corporations to borrow for climate-related activities. Annual reporting regarding allocations and impacts is also produced.

Table 9. Indicators on Climate and Disaster Resilience and Public Expenditure and Fiscal Accountability Assessment Related to Public Financial Management

	Indicator	Bhutan (2023)	Indonesia (2022)	Nepal (2024)	Samoa (2021)
1	Budget alignment with climate change strategies	C	D	B	B
2	Tracking climate-related expenditure	D	C	C	D
3	Climate-responsive budget circular	C	D	B	D
4	Legislative scrutiny	D	D	D	D
5	Climate-responsive public investment management	D+	D+	D	D
6	Climate-responsive non-financial asset management	D	C	D	D
7	Climate-related liabilities	C+	C+	D	D+
8	Climate-responsive public procurement	D+	D+	D	D+
9	Climate-responsive tax administration	B	B	N/A[b]	N/A[b]
10	Compliance of climate-related expenditure	B	B	D	C
11	Climate-responsive fiscal decentralization	C+	C+	C	N/A[c]
12	Climate-related performance information	D	B	C+	C+
13	Climate-related evaluation	C	C	C	D
14	Expenditure outturn for climate actions	N/A[a]	C+	C	N/A[a]

DMC = developing member country, PEFA = public expenditure and fiscal accountability, PFM = public financial management.

Notes:

1. Interpretation of scores:

A: Climate change issues and the policy response are mainstreamed in the relevant PFM institutions, processes, or systems

B: Climate change issues and the policy response are partially mainstreamed in the relevant PFM institutions, processes, or systems

C: Initial efforts have taken place to mainstream climate change issues and the policy response in the relevant PFM institutions, processes, or systems

D: Performance is less than required for a C score

[a] Climate change-related expenditure is not tracked in Bhutan and Samoa.

[b] There are currently no climate-related taxes in place in Nepal and Samoa.

[c] There is no subnational level of government in Samoa.

Source: Climate-related PEFA assessments, various years for the four DMCs.

(b) On ***climate-responsive budget circular***. In Nepal, the budget circular provides a methodology to track climate change-related expenditure. It contains guidance on how to factor climate change mitigation and adaptation expenditure into budget proposals and refers to the national climate change strategies.

(c) On ***climate-related evaluation of expenditure***. Also in Nepal, the Office of Auditor General (OAG) has conducted performance and environment audit of selected climate-related programs in the previous three years and published the reports.

(d) On ***climate-related information in performance plans***. In Samoa, performance indicators by output are provided in the budget document. This includes an indicator directly related to objectives in renewable energy targets; this is submitted to the Legislative Assembly and published. And in Nepal, the major performance indicators by output are included in the budget, including climate change-related outputs. These budget documents are submitted to the legislature and publicly disclosed.

(e) On ***climate-responsive fiscal transfers***. In Indonesia, the SNGs report annually to the central government on the use of climate-related transfers (conditional grants) from the central government.

Table 10. Good Practices in Climate-Related Public Expenditure and Financial Accountability

	Indicators	DMC(s) (Score)	Application Notes
1	9.2. Climate-related tax arrears	Bhutan **(A)** Indonesia **(A)**	**Bhutan:** There is no stock of green tax-related arrears as the taxes are collected in full when imported. **Indonesia:** Luxury goods sales tax arrears was 4.64%.
2	10.1. Effectiveness of the system controls:	Bhutan **(A)** Indonesia **(A)**	**Bhutan:** The government has in place a solid legal and regulatory framework for internal controls, which are also used for climate-related transactions at the commitment and payment stages, and cover all categories of expenditures, including emergency payments. The controls are subject to external audit once a year. **Indonesia:** The regulatory framework describes a system of control for all budgetary central government expenditures, including the climate conditionalities of transactions. A formal commitment control system is introduced through the State Treasury and Budget System. Commitments are also ensured to be in adherence to the budget ceiling. Audits are conducted on an annual basis for all ministries, including for the primary national agency mandated for disaster management.

DMC = developing member country.
Source: CRPFM results for Bhutan, Indonesia, Nepal, and Samoa, for several years (see **Table 9**).

On a related note, the Public Investment Management Assessment (PIMA) for Nepal in 2021 noted that the country has progressively integrated climate change considerations into public investment management framework, but weaknesses remain.[106] While the climate budget coding is used to support the prioritization of climate-relevant capital projects in budget formulation, *ex-post* reviews of projects on climate outcomes are not conducted and climate impact is not integrated into public asset management. These practices are generally in evidence in other selected DMCs as well.[107]

Some Key Issues to Note on Climate and Disaster Resilience & PFM

Climate and Disaster Resilience (CDR) and MTEF. A key point to note is that in countries where MTEF has been in practice and institutionalized, there is a provision for planning based on national climate targets even though some countries may not necessarily have fully configured the information systems needed to support such planning. The same holds true for budget management and execution reporting systems.

Other issues include that of functions related to climate action tending to be largely centralized and the integration of the central government budget with climate strategies and actions still being work in progress. Particularly in countries where subnational governance is gaining prominence specific roles and mandates need to be established across the tiers of government so as to build an effective country platform to respond to ambitious climate targets.

106 International Monetary Fund. 2021b. *Nepal – PIMA Climate Change Module, 2021.* Washington, DC.

107 In particular, the experiences of the Philippines in the broad areas of climate budget tagging are worth exploring here. The country's Department of Budget and Management and the Climate Change Commission have issued provisions on Climate Change Expenditure Tagging (CCET) which aims to track, monitor, and report programs that help address problems posed by climate change. The evidence is then used in the preparation of the national budget. CCET enhances the transparency of tracking budget allotted for climate change purposes. Interestingly, local government units are also mandated to carry out the CCET, which is a clear manifestation of enabling stakeholders at the local level to be more involved in the budgeting process (see, for example, Bicenio and Bangsal, 2016).

CDR and financing. Resource constraints in matters of CDR are always an issue in DMCs. Papua New Guinea demonstrates an example where there is a significant gap between its current climate financing and the estimated requirements.[108] The government in its medium-term development plan, 2023–2027, has allocated a mere 1% of spending (from all sources) to climate finance, which is insufficient to achieve the Enhanced Nationally Determined Contributions, implement the National Action Plan, and support transition to renewable energy. In addition, it is also the ***predictability*** of funding that is a key element of disaster resilience, and particularly at subnational level, and that is missing as well.

What this then means is that, as regards disaster risk financing, insufficient budgetary provisions, operational delays, and a lack of diversified financing instruments for disaster risk reduction, emergency preparedness and response impede the government's ability to prepare for, and respond appropriately to, natural hazard events.

CDR at a policy level. Generally, however, across DMCs, there has been dedicated focus, albeit on ad hoc basis still, on improving the PFM aspects of CDR. For example, in Viet Nam, the World Bank is working with the government to strengthen areas of debt management and disaster risk management. Further, ADB's policy-based programs to the Philippines have tagged reforms in PFM and other governance systems (such as public procurement) so as to holistically address CDR issues at a policy level. Indeed, one of the issues in the Philippines is the degree of policy coherence on CDR given the different development partners that are active in this sphere (these partners include AFD [France], Australia, the European Union, and the World Bank).

CDR and fiscal risks. One particular aspect of CDR work in the selected DMCs, and one related to transparency of information, is the preparation of a fiscal risk register (as in the Philippines); such a register has valuable information on what particular event/policy will have what specific impact(s) on the country's fiscal position. Indeed, since 2012, the Development Budget Coordination Committee has been publishing the government's Fiscal Risk Statement (FRS) to provide a comprehensive view of the country's fiscal exposure from, among others, natural hazards. The FRS is made that much more robust because it also includes information on reforms and risk mitigation efforts, and sensitivity analysis on the impact of changes in key macro-economic variables. In addition, the Department of Budget Management publishes on its website the status of the National Disaster Risk Reduction and Management and Calamity and Quick Response Funds.

Need for transformational focus. ADB's Triple A (Accelerating Atoll Adaptation) initiative to empower the four atoll nations mentioned above (Kiribati, Maldives, the RMI, and Tuvalu) to tackle climate change and secure a resilient future is one of the best examples of a new focus on transformational strategies and way of thinking on how to best address CDR issues. Business-as-usual approaches will clearly not suffice. **Box 18** summarizes the basics of the initiative.

The transformational Triple A initiative has six pillars: (a) risk-informed climate-resilient pathways; (b) transformational adaptation projects; (c) programmatic financing and investments; (d) capacity building; (e) knowledge and innovation; and (f) partnership and coordination. The initiative will be based on the countries' priorities as identified in their national adaptation plans and the assessment of long-term climate risks and possible adaptation pathways.

Triple A will work closely with other ongoing initiatives in these countries, national and regional partners, knowledge institutes, and the private sector—with a strategic focus on long-term planning and adaptation. It is initiatives such as the Triple A that will enable governments in the region to contemplate how they can best incorporate transformational ideas to address issues of climate- and disaster-resilience in their countries.

[108] Department of Foreign Affairs & Trade. 2024. *PNG Climate FIRST (Climate Finance Initiative for Resilience and a Sustainable Transition).*

Box 18. New Narrative on Transformational Approaches to Address Climate and Disaster Resilience Issues

The narrative of the need for transformational adaptation starts with some basic facts:

- Short-term responses are needed for immediate relief; facing long-term challenges, however, requires something more long-term and fundamentally different (termed "transformational").
- This requires understanding of, and fuller information on, current and future climate risks.
- These risks must then be prioritized.
- For which integrated, and sequenced adaptation investments across sectors will be necessary. The key here is to ensure that there is no maladaptation (i.e., the right project but the wrong application).

Several elements will need to be considered closely in instituting measures that will be transformational: (a) holistic strategies are needed (i.e., those that bring together science, inclusive governance approaches, local cultural and traditional knowledge, and innovative financing mechanisms); (b) a whole-of-government approach is needed (given that climate and disaster relief issues are rarely uni-dimensional); (c) as resources are biding constraints,[a] efforts will need to be made to secure adequate levels of funding; and (d) a much longer planning time horizon will be needed, which implies governments' credible commitment to last over many programming and election cycles.

[a] For example, Giardino maintains that implementing the RMI's National Adaptation Plan will mean total costs equivalent to 17.8 times the country's GDP in 2023 for a 0.5-meter sea level rise; the amounts balloon to 125 times if the scenario is a 2-meter sea level rise.

Source: A. Giardino. 2025. *Navigating the Rising Tide: Transformational Adaptation for Resilient Atoll Nations* (https://development.asia/insight/navigating-rising-tide-transformational-adaptation-resilient-atoll-nations; (accessed 21 August 2025).

Institutionalizing Gender Equality and Social Inclusion

Introduction

Gender equality and social inclusion (GESI) matters occupy a central role in any discussion on not only development objectives but also their component parts such as PFM. Also, target 16.7 of the SDGs (on ensuring "responsive, inclusive, participatory, and representative decision-making at all levels") alludes to gender equality in all facets of life and bringing to the fore marginalized populations in the decision-making fora at all levels of government of government.

GESI issues at country level can be considered from various angles, including: (a) the principle of equality and non-discrimination as may be detailed in a country's constitution; (b) constitutional national commissions and other institutions; (c) various fundamental rights of individuals and groups (for example, right to equality); (d) positive provisions on, for example, affirmative action or a policy of "leave no one behind";[109] (e) protection of women from different forms of violence, exploitation, or discrimination; and (f) the rights of specific disadvantaged groups to participate in the functions of the state and equal access to public services.

[109] When Member States adopted the SDGs as their own development goals they also pledged to 'leave no one behind' and to "endeavour to reach the furthest behind first." What this means is that governments will make dedicated efforts to 'fast-track' efforts to help those that are the furthest behind and most marginalized (UNDP. n.d. *What Does It Mean to Leave No One Behind? A Framework for Implementation* (https://www.undp.org/sites/g/files/zskgke326/files/publications/Brochure_LNOB_web.pdf; accessed 19 August 2025).

At a policy and strategy level, any GESI measure needs to consider two approaches: (a) through mainstreaming, and/or (b) through targeted interventions. More broadly, a government's Gender Equality Policy generally prioritizes: (a) the economic empowerment of women; (b) their meaningful participation in all parts of society (e.g., in the civil service, or elected office); and (c) the elimination of gender-based violence and harmful practices.

Particular emphasis is placed on developing gender accountable systems in all tiers of governments (including down to the grassroots level) through laws and policy provisions, institutional mechanisms, and capacity building. There is also a general understanding that causes of exclusion are structurally embedded in society, thus taking longer to change.

Focus on Inclusiveness

The concept of gender equality is rather hollow without consideration of the broader value of inclusiveness. In Nepal, for example, a core part of the move to federalism was inclusiveness, not just on the gender front but broadly at the social level as well. All the work on GESI in Nepal at present (and primarily at central level for now) has had these attributes:

(a) The strategies and guidelines encompass a wide swathe of marginalized populations, including *Dalits* (or untouchables), and Muslims.
(b) The primary focus is on the need to identify, and mitigate, barriers faced by these populations in accessing resources, information, and opportunities.
(c) Emphasizing new modalities, for example, a focus on behavior change in the broader society.
(d) Ensuring service delivery improvements to these population groups as a central plank of national public policy.
(e) Reservations in decision-making positions at all levels.
(f) Capacity development for these population groups so that they can sustain efforts to be included in the mainstream.

A key part of the debate and discussion on GESI centers on the universal value of leave no one behind. While it focuses on everything from eradicating poverty in all its forms to ending discrimination, it resonates particularly with ensuring that governments are purposefully working towards minimizing exclusion, inequalities, and vulnerabilities that leave people—but particularly marginalized people—behind and undermine their potential. It also asks of governments to address the root causes of such exclusion.

Concept of Intersectionality

It is in this context that the concept of intersectionality must be brought up on issues of GESI. Considerations of equality and inclusiveness need to be viewed from a perspective that brings together the myriad forces that determine how marginalized populations need to navigate the public space to, for example, access available opportunities or to exercise their agency. Across many DMCs the GESI polices – and their practices – do not seem to demonstrate to any extent that there is application, or sometimes even a true understanding, of the concept of intersectionality.

The concept illustrates that there is an interplay among various elements/conditions that govern the space for action by marginalized populations. These elements generally include gender, race, ethnicity, age, class, sexual identity, religion, spatial location, etc. This makes giving effect to GESI policies as part of broader governance reforms greater complexity.

Mainstreaming GESI. This term has also been used widely in the DMCs, with general consensus around what it means. Internalizing GESI considerations in all cycles of policies, programs, and processes (e.g., project identification, implementation, and monitoring and evaluation) need to be matched by continuously developing, updating, and curating indicators, measures, and standards for gender and development.

GESI mainstreaming is across many fronts, for example, climate action, or governance. Actions taken to address the adverse effects of climate change (both adaptation and mitigation) will have significant effects on gender transformation. High levels of gender inequality (measured by, e.g., the UN's Gender Inequality Index) tend to show a higher degree of vulnerability to the negative impacts of climate change (i.e., imposing greater constrains on women and marginalized populations to manage the situation or to minimize adverse effects on them).

As for strengthening governance as part of GESI mainstreaming, the focus has been on comprehensive assessments of national plans, policies, institutions, and budgets, to assess gender and other social gaps, and then to identify concrete and practical actions to close these gaps. More importantly, the allocation of dedicated resources needs to be matched by robust monitoring protocols that systematically measure progress in reducing discrimination and exclusion and that identify clear actions to be taken to remedy the adverse situation.

GESI Issues vis-à-vis PFM

One such aspect of GESI mainstreaming can be seen with respect to PFM and how efforts coalesce around whether the PFM system effectively caters to adequate resources being channeled to marginalized groups and how they are done so. In many countries governmental agencies have been mandated to report on gender-responsive budgeting (GRB) provisions for each program head in their budgeting and program system. This ensures that issues on GRB, at least at this level, are mainstreamed.

However, across most countries, there exists a policy-to-budget gap. Data indicate that, while 92% of countries have gender equality policies and laws, only 53% have clear budget allocations for gender equality programs.[110] This lack of resources renders policies ineffective. The solution is adherence to principles of, and actions in, GRB, which is the core mechanism for integrating gender into PFM. It involves incorporating a gender perspective into the entire budget cycle: planning, allocation, execution, and evaluation. The key to successful GRB is to institutionalize it within existing systems, making it a standard part of the process rather than an additional or external burden.

The mechanisms to enhance GESI in the PFM system can also be seen in the work of entities such as a Gender Responsive Budgeting Committee in the MOF given that it issues system-wide guidance on GRB. The integration of the GRB principles in any budget management information system is an instrumental step of governments in the area of GESI. Actions that governments are taking on enhancing GESI with respect to PFM also include: (a) directives for gender equality and women's empowerment integration in the government's functions and programs; (b) improvements on gender disaggregated performance information for service delivery; and (c) consideration of gender-impact analysis of budget policy decisions and gender-aligned MTEF. What appears to be missing, however, generally is a strong outcome M&E mechanism, something that the supplementary framework for assessing gender-responsive PFM in the PEFA has continually highlighted.[111]

GESI mainstreaming also has a subnational element, particularly in the PFM space, because local governments need to effectively integrate GESI in their respective development planning and budgeting processes. This reform consideration is increasingly gaining traction, especially in the area of local government disaster risk reduction and management. For example, the Philippines has recognized the key role that local governments play in disaster response, and that some of the issues women face at the local level during disasters are: (a) increased vulnerability to gender-based violence; (b) compromised sexual and reproductive health services, and psychosocial counseling;

110 UNECE. 2024. "UNECE regional report highlights the need for more progress in women's economic rights and elimination of gender-based violence" (https://unece.org/gender/press/unece-regional-report-highlights-need-more-progress-womens-economic-rights-and; accessed: 10 January 2026).

111 The PEFA supplementary framework for assessing gender-responsive PFM is a set of nine indicators that measure the degree to which a country's PFM systems address the government's goals with regard to acknowledging different needs of men and women, and different subgroups of these categories, and promoting gender equality. The framework can be applied at both national and subnational levels.

(c) a lack of gender-responsive facilities and products; (d) increased unpaid care and community work; and (e) limited mobility and skills typically taught to men, such as swimming and climbing, thereby hindering their self-rescue and self-defense capabilities.

Furthermore, the government also discovered that women are underrepresented in disaster risk reduction and management processes, including decision-making, designing, planning, budgeting, implementing and monitoring programs, which contributes to their vulnerability and low adaptive capacity in the face of climate and disaster risks. This highlights the importance of capacity building and guidance on gender-responsive local government planning and disaster-related derivative plans, and of establishing effective engagement mechanisms with community-level CSOs.

Some Key Issues to Note on GESI and PFM

Gender-responsive PFM. While not all DMCs may have undertaken the Gender Responsive PFM (GRPFM) assessments, for those that have (e.g., Nepal, Indonesia, Tonga), the messages that emerge are quite clear. For example, the one conducted in Nepal in 2024 indicates that it has strong gender equality and women's empowerment-related commitments. It also has directives for gender equality and women's empowerment integration in the government's functions and programs even as it needs to improve on gender disaggregated performance information for service delivery and consider gender-impact analysis of budget policy decisions, and gender-aligned MTEF. For this, it needs to have a strong outcome M&E mechanism.

Table 11 lists those DMCs that scored a B in the GRPFM assessments.[112] The score shows that the DMC has partially mainstreamed into the relevant PFM institution, process, or system that particular element on gender-responsive PFM.

Table 11. Sub-Indicators on Gender-Responsive Public Financial Management in Developing Member Countries[a]

(Sub)Indicator & Descriptor		DMCs
1.1.	Gender impact analysis of expenditure policy proposals	Tonga
2.1.	Gender-responsive public investment management	Nauru
3.1.	Gender-responsive budget circular	Indonesia
4.1.	Gender-responsive budget proposal documentation	Indonesia, Nauru
5.1.	Sex-disaggregated performance plans for service delivery	Bhutan, Tonga
5.2.	Sex-disaggregated performance achieved for service delivery	Bhutan
6.1.	Tracking budget expenditure for gender equality	Indonesia, Nepal
7.1.	Gender-responsive reporting	Bhutan
8.1.	Evaluation of gender impacts of service delivery	Tonga

DMC = developing member country, PFM = public financial management.

Notes:

1. Interpretation of a B Score: "gender impact analysis is partially mainstreamed into the relevant PFM institution(s), process(es), or system(s)'

[a] The table lists DMCs that had a B score (the highest achieved by any DMC to date in the GRPFM assessments). These are DMCs whose assessment results were made public.

Source: Gender-Responsive PEFA assessments, various years for the six DMCs.

[112] These are: Bhutan (2023), Georgia (2022), Indonesia (2020), Nauru (2022), Nepal (2024), and Tonga (2020). Interestingly, none of these six DMCs scored even a B+ in any of the nine indicators of the GRPFM assessment, or even on a sub-set of them (i.e., within the gender dimensions). As such, a B score is deemed to reflect a good practice for purposes of this study.

Two main conclusions stand out here: (a) no DMC (of those covered in this study) has been able to score an A in any of the (sub)indicators (an A score shows that the DMC has mainstreamed a particular gender element in the PFM system); and (b) only nine of the 12 sub-indicators feature on which some of the DMCs were able to score a B. Three critical ones that are missing (i.e., no DMC scored even a B on them) are: (a) gender impact analysis of revenue policy proposals; (b) gender-responsive legislative scrutiny of budgets; and (c) gender-responsive legislative scrutiny of audit reports. All three missing ones are significant.

These are indeed serious gaps; the evidence shows that PFM systems in DMCs are still gender-nonresponsive. As such, it is difficult to meaningfully talk of GESI mainstreaming in their PFM systems.[113]

Gender responsiveness and access. One primary cause for such gender unresponsiveness is undoubtedly the continued presence of issues of exclusion, which imply that governments should place emphasis on ensuring that marginalized populations have access to information, resources, opportunities, and can exercise their agency. These are linearly higher orders of action to take. Many DMCs may have made meaningful inroads to providing information to these populations (and, in parallel, collated information and their needs and attributes in censuses, for example), providing greater and easier access to resources is something that still needs more attention.

On opportunities. On the third element (that of access to opportunities) governments clearly need to place greater attention. For example, DMCs (Nepal, Bangladesh, Viet Nam, to name a few) may have mandated a particular threshold of representation for women and other marginalized populations in national and local bodies but that does not necessarily translate to them being given opportunities to speak up at deliberative meetings or to have meaningful roles in decision-making processes.

Exercise of agency. Finally, it is on the matter of women and marginalized populations being able to exercise their agency that DMCs still seem to have a long way to go. The ability of members of these population groups to define their own goals, to act on them, and to influence their own lives is constrained across countries. The degree of that constraint may vary but the issue remains substantive.

Reinforcing Oversight and Accountability, with Extensions to Integrity

Introduction

One of the key components of good governance has always been that of accountability (that is, answerability for work carried out, resources expended, processes followed, and *ex-ante* stated results achieved). This is facilitated by strong oversight provisions and mechanisms in the countries. These can be found in PFM as well as various other systems, such as, for example:

(a) Financial and corporate sector: for example, Securities and Exchange Commission (in DMCs such as Philippines, and Sri Lanka).
(b) Market competition: Competition Commission (e.g., in Indonesia, Viet Nam).

[113] In countries outside the Asia and Pacific region that have successfully juxtaposed GESI outcomes with budgeting (such as Mexico) measures have been put in place to ensure a clear shift from merely tracking spending inputs to demanding transformative results-based outcomes viewed with a gender lens. In Mexico, resource allocation to specifically reduce gender gaps are specified in an annex of the Federal Expenditure Budget. Indeed, the gender agenda has been a focus of the budget for over 20 years now, with stipulations for the same formalized through legal mandates and institutional arrangements. The institutional framework of the budget process in Mexico allows for cross-cutting tracking of public investments with a particular focus on intersectionality, for example, connecting gender equality with climate action and social inclusion; Patel et al. 2021.

(c) Sectors: for example, (a) telecom sector: for example, Communications Authority of Maldives; (b) electric power sector: for example, the Nepal Electricity Authority; (c) media sector: for example, Pakistan Electronic Media Regulatory Authority.
(d) Public sector procurement domain: for example, PPMO (Nepal).

This study puts forth a particularly reformulated way of looking at issues of oversight and accountability. It argues for a more whole-of-government, and therefore more enhanced and refined, approach to considering issues of good governance implied in the concept of oversight and accountability, that is, it argues for an integrity system as a fundamental element of good governance.

On Oversight

To begin with, the study briefly reviews the oversight functions in the overall governance domain, where functions are evident across several areas. These are relevant to note so as to set the contextual background more comprehensively.

Oversight and role of constitutional bodies. The role of constitutional bodies such as the OAG in Nepal is in instituting rigorous audit of use of public resources. By and large, the audit reports of this Office, which are tabled in the legislature, get substantive attention, as is the case in other selected DMCs too. The work on legislative oversight (e.g., that provided by the PAC in the Fiji legislature) on government expenditures through primarily robust review of the audit reports needs to be specifically highlighted.

Oversight during the budget process. The oversight provided by, for example, MOF includes possible roles of the central entities such as the Planning Commission, or the Fiscal Commission in terms of resource flow as part of the central grants system. In the Philippines, for example, the external audit functions of the COA provide ample oversight during the budget process, including the planning and implementation stages.

Oversight provided by use of systems. Such oversight, and strict adherence to standards that mandate specific actions, are critical in all selected DMCs. For example, in Bangladesh, it is argued that enhancing the iBAS++, integrating it with the treasury single account (TSA), adopting IPSAS Cash Basis of Accounting, and improving the timeliness of annual reporting have substantially improved oversight in the macrofiscal environment.

Policy oversight. Policy oversight is provided by a central agency that is close to the head of government, for example, the Office of Prime Minister and Cabinet of Ministers in Nepal. Its oversight functions include, among others, regulatory impact assessment so as to ensure that policies being recommended for approval by Cabinet are not in conflict with others (either already in place or being actively considered).

Administrative oversight. In some DMCs, this is provided by the Office of the Prime Minister, which also ensures that policy implementation takes place in an effective and inclusive manner. In the Kyrgyz Republic, the Cabinet of Ministers recently established a National Institute for Strategic Initiatives whose mandates include, among others, regulatory framework optimization (to reduce excessive regulations) and provision of broad oversight over state actions to eliminate redundant structures and accelerate decision-making processes.

Oversight of public procurement. This is a critical component of any government's financial system (given that public funds are provided for purposes of delivery of goods, services, and works). In light of the criticality of getting the procurement system right to avoid leakages and malfeasance in the use of public funds, governments have taken deep interest in ensuring proper oversight of procurement systems. For example, the role played by the Fiji Procurement Office also includes the conduct of compliance assessments of procurement functions and activities across the whole of government. In Azerbaijan, the State Service for Antimonopoly and Consumer

Market Control – under the Ministry of Economy and the regulatory body for public procurement – also plays an observer role during biddings, investigates controversies related to procurement, and carries out the contract execution oversight role as well.

Oversight on monetary policy. Such oversight is provided by entities such as the central bank on monetary policy work, or the securities exchange boards on financial markets. For example, Mongolbank (the Central Bank of Mongolia) – through its Monetary Policy Department – exercises an oversight role in this sector through preparation of the monetary policy guidelines for the upcoming year and also development of a macro-prudential policy framework.

Oversight of anticorruption work. Anticorruption bodies use their oversight powers to ensure that government work is being carried out in an ethical manner with no recourse to corrupt activities. In some countries, such as Nepal, they are constitutional bodies and have significant powers.[114] **Table 12** shows six forms of anticorruption agencies in the selected DMCs; the Commission form of organization is the most common.

Table 12. Forms of Anticorruption Agencies in Selected Developing Member Countries

	Type	DMC, and Name of Agency
1	**Commission**[a]	*Bangladesh, Timor-Leste* – Anticorruption Commission *Fiji, Papua New Guinea* – Independent Commission Against Corruption *Nepal* – Commission for the Prevention of Abuse of Authority *Philippines* – Presidential Anticorruption Commission *Sri Lanka* – Commission to Investigate Allegations of Bribery or Corruption
2	**Authority**	*Mongolia* – Independent Authority Against Corruption *Lao PDR* – State Inspection and Anticorruption Authority
3	**Agency**	*Uzbekistan* – Anticorruption Agency
4	**Organizational Unit**	*Kiribati* – Public Service Integrity and Corruption Control Unit under the Public Service Office
5	**Council**	*Kyrgyz Republic* – Anticorruption Business Council (under the President)
6	**Committee**	*Viet Nam* – Central Steering Committee on Anticorruption and Wrong-doings

DMC = developing member country, Lao PDR = Lao People's Democratic Republic.

Note:

[a] Turkmenistan's Interdepartmental Coordination Anticorruption Commission (established in September 2020) is a slight variation on the Commission in that it works based on a charter approved by the President, comprises members of law enforcement and other government bodies, and implements an (unpublished) plan to combat corruption.

Source: review of various documents.

On paper most of these (with the exception of the organizational unit in Kiribati) are at the apex of the organizational system for purposes of authority and mandates to address and manage the corruption problem in the country. However, their organization design implies differences in resourcing, procedures of work, etc. The primary attribute expected of these bodies is that they are independent, both in terms of how they operate, and in terms of funding sources. However, due to severe capacity constraints, their work on oversight of anticorruption work is uniformly constrained.[115]

114 Interestingly, the ACC Reform Commission in Bangladesh recently recommended that the country's Anticorruption Commission be recognized as a constitutional body so as to be made more independent and potentially, as a result, more powerful. This is not to say that the transition to a constitutional body would necessarily improve matters; the experiences of the Commission for the Investigation of Abuse of Authority (a constitutional body) in neighboring Nepal would attest to this.

115 Largely to address this gap in Maldives, the President in late 2023 inaugurated the Maldives National Anticorruption Academy, a unit within the ACC tasked to educate, train, and develop human resources to investigate economic crimes and corruption. The Academy is still in its infancy and much work remains to be done, such as on developing required programs for delivery.

Oversight and CSOs. CSOs and others do institute some discipline on how public policy is being implemented on the ground (their work, e.g., in social audits is symptomatic of this). In Bangladesh, the CSO Alliance (an umbrella organization that brings together NGOs, CSOs, social enterprises, and others) has taken a keen interest in advocacy for transparency in government at all levels. In all selected DMCs, at the most basic level, CSOs are active in ensuring effective service delivery at the local level. However, in some countries (such as Nepal) the civic space (i.e., the operating environment for CSOs) is deemed to be constrained.

As is clear, there are various instances of the practice of oversight in the governance system in countries. The primary intent in all of them has always been to ensure that there is a robust public overview of the use and accounting of public funds and state actions. There is also now evidence of a shift in the thinking of oversight and accountability from compliance-based measures to proactive risk-informed public financial governance.

On Accountability

The second integral and a resultant component of oversight (i.e., accountability) should be viewed from four core perspectives:

(a) *Accountability of results* i.e., that governments are held answerable for achieving the results they had promised, *ex ante;* this relates to effectiveness of government action.
(b) *Accountability of resource use* i.e., answerability to the public on how the resources were used in producing the results and whether there were efficiency measures put in place for such use.
(c) *Accountability of adherence to rules, regulations, and processes* i.e., ensuring that all the work that governments do is within set regulatory and policy boundaries, and that all actions are legal; this relates to the legality aspect of government action.
(d) *Accountability of broader governance norms,* such as transparency, inclusiveness (of social, gender, and other forms); this relates to equity dimensions of government action.

Some of the more serious issues that have been highlighted in the analytical work in recent years in the areas of oversight and accountability have centered on capacity gaps and other associated vulnerabilities and weaknesses, or of the responsibility of oversight functions scattered across government agencies with inadequate coordination. **Box 19** exemplifies these issues with respect to selected weaknesses and gaps in anticorruption work in Nepal.

On Roles of Civil Society Organizations

No discussion on oversight and accountability at the country level is complete without a treatment of the role that CSOs play in the process of ensuring such oversight. On service delivery, in particular, CSOs and religious groups (for example, churches in Papua New Guinea)[116] have always assumed important roles, particularly for the marginalized and vulnerable populations. The key role for traditional leaders has also been recognized; in the Pacific, for example, governments assign import to community involvement and local culture given the existence of tight knit communities. In general, CSOs play a key role in ensuring that governments are accountable, and governments have understood this. **Table 13** documents some notes on the work of CSOs across a select group of DMCs.

There is increasing awareness and appreciation now in all DMCs of the role that CSOs play in governance. Enabling them to have better access to information would meaningfully fulfill such roles. Public policies related to the work of CSOs, and regulatory provisions giving effect to them, are at times deemed to be restrictive, which means that CSOs have not been able to be as effective as is possible in many DMCs.

116 Indeed, Papua New Guinea's Vision 2050 calls for increasing the role of churches in the provision of basic health services and provision of basic education services as well with respect to secondary and vocational schools.

Box 19. Selected Weaknesses and Gaps in the Oversight of Anticorruption Work in Nepal

1. **Procurement related:**
   (a) Corruption possibilities in abnormally low bids, and systemic provision for acceptance of such bids
   (b) Users' Committees tend to make payments as commission for securing procurement contracts.

2. **Capacity of oversight agencies**, for example, lack of analytical and research capacity in relevant parliamentary bodies to better address corruption and malgovernance issues.

3. **Institutional weaknesses:**
   (a) Poor compliance of directives (from parliamentary committees, CIAA, NVC, OAG, PPMO, etc.)
   (b) General inability of NVC to carry out its mandates, for example, high staff turnover ratio, lack of quasi-judicial powers, inability to carry out technical audits in major government projects)
   (c) Continued practice of lump-sum allocations under the miscellaneous category in budgets, leading to misallocation of resources with little transparency
   (d) Responsibility of oversight functions scattered across government agencies with inadequate coordination
   (e) Lack of CIAA jurisdiction to banks, financial institutions, cooperatives, and the private sector.

4. **Weaknesses at subnational level**, for example, capacity gaps and low political will in SNGs for the fight against corruption. Also, there is need for strengthening the delegation of authority to Chief District Officers at the local level so that they are better able to carry out their anticorruption functions.

CIAA = Commission for the Investigation of Abuse of Authority; NVC = National Vigilance Center; OAG = Office of the Auditor General; PPMO = Public Procurement Monitoring Office; SNGs = subnational governments.
Source: various reports from CIAA and NVC, cited in the country diagnostic work for the Nepal CPS, 2024.

Some Key Issues on Oversight and Accountability

Moving away from a linear view of accountability. In the practice of governance across the DMCs, there is almost a linear process of considering issues of oversight and accountability – basically, that once there is proper oversight of public action, robust accountability will result in the public sector, which will then facilitate holding to account those that are engaged in malgovernance (for example, engaged in corruption). This has now been deemed to be a simplistic formulation.

Appeal of a National Integrity System. Increasingly, there is a need felt to elevate the nature of the discussion on good governance and anticorruption in countries towards consideration of a National Integrity System (NIS).[117] This will ensure that a broader set of principles, action frames, and a whole-of-government approach are taken into consideration. Experiences from countries where a NIS has been instituted (such as Bangladesh and Indonesia) show that focusing on a more holistic way of thinking of enhancing ethics and integrity[118] in the public sector is superior to a more narrow-focused approach to just combating corruption.

[117] This section draws from the internal country diagnostic work for the Nepal CPS, 2024, in itself drawing generously from OECD. 2017. Recommendation of the Council on Public Integrity (accessed 20 August 2025). OECD's work in this area is treated as a global benchmark for jurisdictions to adhere to, particularly since its application is not country- or context-specific. This concept has been worked on before in ADB's engagement with the Government of Bangladesh as part of broader reform efforts on governance (see, for example, ADB's Good Governance Program in Bangladesh, 2008).

[118] While ethics and integrity are often used interchangeably, there is a subtle difference: ethics refers to broad principles and a code of conduct which dictate how individuals and institutions need to interact; integrity, on the other hand, refers to the actual practices of such ethical conduct. Thus, the focus on integrity brings out a more practical aspect to good governance.

Table 13. Notes on Civil Society Organization Engagement in Select Developing Member Countries

	Developing Member Country	Example of Civil Society Organization Engagement
1	**Georgia**	• Well-established CSOs, as well as local branches of international NGOs, have built ties with the executive and legislative branches of government, and been providing training and capacity-building services for the government, the media, and other CSOs. • CSOs have had multiple platforms for engagement with government, and have helped produce policy documents, draft laws, research reports and recommendations regarding government policies. They also contributed to the process of drafting Georgia's anticorruption strategy and action plans and help monitor their implementation. • CSOs are wary of accessing various available government grants due to concerns about the politicization of grant-making mechanisms.
2	**Mongolia**	• Most of the existing non-profit organizations focus on training, research, counseling, aid and care services and advocacy for the well-being of the public, communities, youth, children, women, and families. • The legal framework for CSOs and NGOs has generated some confusion, largely centered on the regulatory regime for these organizations and on different types of legal entities falling under different laws. • The government is working on the establishment of a Civil Society Development Council which will have substantial powers over NGO operations (including a directive from the NGOs to submit annual reports detailing their funding, among others). • CSOs generally monitor policies and regulations rather than actively engage in policymaking/dialogue.
3	**Nepal**	• The general perception on civil society engagement is that politics has now co-opted CSOs, and this politicization of the civic space has constrained its effectiveness. Indeed, it is fair to say that CSOs' independence appears to be declining as they are increasingly (although not uniformly) perceived to be aligned with political parties. • As such, Nepal's civic space is "obstructed" despite the open political space created by the new 2015 Constitution.
4	**Philippines**	• The vast network of CSOs not only actively participates in policy-making bodies but also directly works on public service delivery programs of agencies, including a conditional cash transfer program and a program to ensure the availability and affordability of food in communities with low-income families. • CSOs are critically present in governance-related activities (e.g., participatory budgeting through the Budget Partnership Agreements, which are legal instruments that define a mechanism for a CSO's formal engagement in budget preparation and execution at the agency level); public procurement monitoring; and participatory audit through the COA's technical audit system as members of the audit team.

COA = Commission on Audit, CSO = civil society organization, NGO = nongovernment organization.

Source: ADB; information on CSOs in Mongolia is from Civil Society Consortium and SICA. 2021. *Exploring the Current State of Civic Space and Identifying Its Need for a Favourable Legal Environment*. Full Report. Ulaanbaatar.

The relevance and importance of elevating the conversation from oversight and accountability to integrity is best brought out in the results of the 2023 Integrity Assessment Survey in Indonesia, carried out by KPK (*Komisi Pemberantasan Korupsi*, or Corruption Eradication Commission). The results showed that system improvements through service digitalization are not enough to curb corruption and should thus be accompanied by improvements in the integrity and ethical standards of relevant stakeholders (employees, service users, supervisors, etc.).

System-wide focus on ethics. To date, a great amount of work of development partners and governments in DMCs have focused on trying to address the problem of corruption and resource mismanagement in the country through an approach that can be labeled as institution or actor-focused (e.g., supporting the work of the country's

Table 14. Moving from Oversight and Accountability to a National Integrity System (Generalized Set)

Moving from...	Moving to a Focus on... ...
Set 1: The executive (e.g., the public procurement agency)	Roles of constitutional, legislative, and judiciary bodies including, for example, the Office of Auditor General, Public Accounts Committee, and Special Courts mandated to look at ethics cases; also political parties
Set 2: The government	Roles of individuals, civil society organizations, media, private sector, etc. (including industry associations as well as individual firms and companies)
Set 3: The central government	Roles of subnational governments (even as they are undergoing rapid restructuring, for example, in Viet Nam, at the moment)
Set 4: Controlling for extrinsic acts of corruption (e.g., bribery)	To the intrinsic acts (e.g., influence trading), that is, consider any act of malgovernance as a contributory element to eroding public integrity.

Note:
The focus here is on taking a look at something that transcends a simple or transactional act (such as graft) to something that may be influencing or enabling such a situation in the first place (for example, weak and undemocratic political parties). The notion of 'intersectionality' is an integral part of the point being made here.
Source: Country diagnostic work for the Nepal CPS, 2024.

anticorruption agency) or ensuring that the e-procurement system is robust and not susceptible to corrupt and unethical practices. What appears to be less emphasized is a system-wide focus on assessing the feasibility of institutions as well as systems to promote ethics in the public service.

The bottom line is the acceptance that the fight against corruption cannot be won by prosecution alone or by more rules, stricter compliance, or tougher enforcement; the necessary and sufficient condition for such effective action is to take into account all these provisions along with an inclusive approach based on values, ethics, and integrity in the public sector.

Moving towards NIS. Because the NIS asks that the bigger picture be taken into account, there is a transition implied from the traditional areas of focus to the broader frontier; thus, we can speak of a move away for governments across four sets to take into account while considering application of NIS (see **Table 14**, with generic application to DMCs in the region).

Table 14 makes the very strong point that DMCs and development partners should actively consider how best to move to a more holistic manner of considering ways to address of malgovernance robustly. Consequently, the focus on integrity is a more elevated approach to good governance, which takes a systemic, holistic, and whole-of-government approach to governance. The experiences of frontier DMCs in the region (for example, Bhutan, in the area of governance) lends credence to this proposed new way of thinking.

Part D. Pathways for Reforms

Introduction

The deliberations across the nine emerging themes in ADB's and DMCs' work on PSMG and the use of country systems in the report bring out some very consistent themes which are worth reiterating as the discussions veer to the pathways (or opportunities) for reforms. This section will benefit from a recap of the stylized results chain (Figure 2, p. 9).

The three main components in the results chain can be viewed as consisting of three vectors (or opportunities): (a) on systemic outcomes; (b) on strategic priorities; and (c) on instrumentation to give effect to the other two vectors of relevant elements. Contextualizing the focus on these three vectors are conclusions that have emerged from a review of the issues/challenges as well as good practices in various DMCs, as well as concepts that help frame the discussions in their proper light. For example, the study argues that clearly underlying the root cause(s) of malgovernance (such as on fiscal risks) is lack of fiscal transparency, which itself is a function of the absence or incompleteness of data and information and its access. These points are detailed in this section, and relevant conclusions are then drawn to the four specific frames of action that ADB and the DMCs could consider in improving good governance.

Narrative on Malgovernance and Downstream Risks

A review of the discussions on PFM systems in operation currently in the DMCs of the Asia and Pacific region, shows several gaps and, more importantly, allows us to identify the nature of some downstream risks of malgovernance (**Table 15**).

Table 15 brings out much more than a litany of gaps in the PFM systems in DMCs. What it does is provide the backdrop to the nature of reforms needed for the systems to be more robust. These actions form the core of the three vectors mentioned above.

Discussions on the Backdrops to Reform Actions

To be able to critically frame the actions of governments to the nine themes reviewed here, and to be able to also demarcate the appropriate reform space in the countries, two main considerations serve as appropriate backdrops. These have been taken for granted in all the development work being carried out. They do get highlighted at times in specific action plans of specific sectors, but not putting them in their right frame will do injustice to any reform attempts.

Table 15. Stylized Narrative on Malgovernance Stemming from Weak Public Financial Management Systems

	Gaps in PFM System	Nature of Downstream Risks of Malgovernance
1	Compromised budgetary framework resulting from: (a) absence of ministry-level medium-term aggregate expenditure ceilings, (b) misalignment of expenditure proposals with strategic plans, (c) inefficient allocation of resources due to unrealistic budgets, and (d) inadequate integration of capital expenditure with ODA funds	• Opportunities for misappropriation and misuse of public resources
2	Lack of public participation in budget preparation	• Budgetary process susceptible to the risk of manipulation for personal benefit or for the gain of particular factions or agendas
3	Inefficiencies in the treasury system, as evident in, among others: (a) absence of a mechanism to track the time for billing statements to be submitted and for payment orders to be issued; and (b) practice of consolidating several types of expenses under a single payment order	• Offering of bribes to expedite the payment process • Solicitation of bribes by government officials in exchange for fast-tracking payment orders • Risk of fraudulent activities such as duplicate payments, overpayments or the payment of false invoices, etc.
4	Lack of transparency in expenditures for projects due to a lack of a single system for accounting and recording expenditures	• Potential malgovernance risk results from fragmented and uncoordinated systems that can create opportunities for misreporting or manipulation of financial information
5	Lack of formal quality assurance processes in internal audits and weak compliance of agencies in submitting internal audit reports hinder the effectiveness of oversight mechanisms.	• Opportunities for corrupt practices such as the misuse of public resources or other forms of malfeasance
6	Weak accountability, and lack of trust in, public procurement system resulting from, for example: (a) preferential use of direct contracting for capital expenditures, (b) absence of robust databases for cost estimation and procurement transactions, and (c) contract price variations beyond allowed thresholds	• Increases procurement-related corruption risks, such as tailored requirements for favored bidders, undetected collusion or fraudulent activities, unwarranted increases in contract prices, and uncontested unfair and biased decisions.
7	The absence of an e-procurement system and CSO monitoring of public procurement activities are also gaps that open the procurement system to corruption-related risks that result from a lack of transparency	• Non-transparent processes yield opportunities for favoritism, kickbacks, other forms of corruption, lack of competition, and inefficient expenditures as part of a weak public procurement system

CSO = civil society organization, ODA = overseas development assistance, PFM = public financial management.
Source: Authors.

Information Lapses, Non-Disclosure, and Asymmetry

A detailed review of the macrofiscal and governance issues in DMCs shows that the core of the causes of the lapses in the PFM and other systems of how governments carry out their functions is what has been described as information asymmetry. This has many layers; **Figure 11** is an attempt to conceptualize the main points to be made, juxtaposed with examples of lapses and good practices in evidence from among DMCs in the region.

In Figure 11, and related to it, note the following:

(a) Data and information are the underlying building blocks of not only the development policies but also the implementation work of the same (for example, monitoring of development projects inherently implies reliance on the criticality of appropriate data, databases, and information systems that enable such data to be used and remain in the public domain). This particular focus on data and information includes collection, curation, storage, and usage of the same.

Figure 11. Conceptualizing the Centrality of Evidence in Policy and Implementation

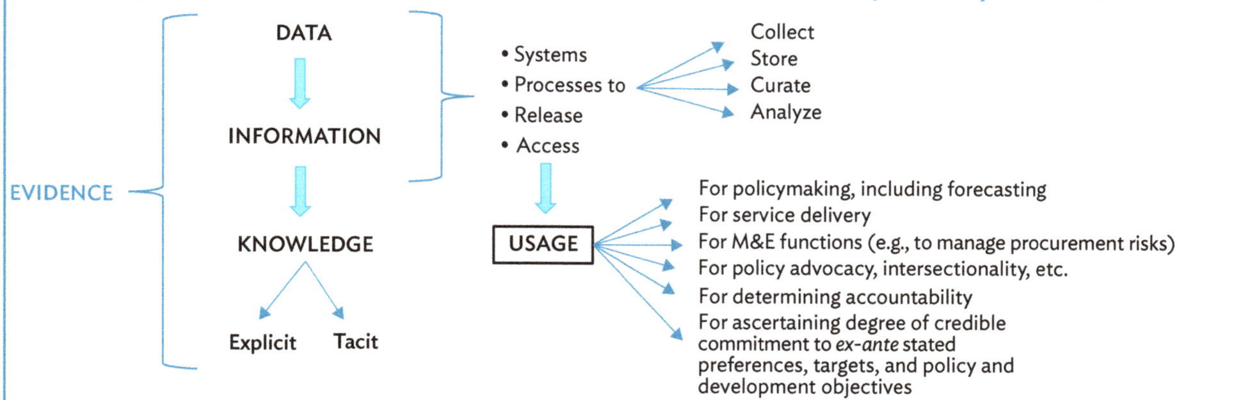

Select Evidence of Lapses

- Financial reports from sub-national governments rarely published
- Contingent PPP liabilities not disclosed in budget documents
- Little data-driven monitoring of procurement
- Inadequate information on *Swakelola* (self-managed procurement)
- Inadequate public information on use of extra-budgetary sources at union and state levels

Select Evidence of Good Practices

- Extended service of the National Statistical Office must be established in each province
- Comprehensive information on each of the phases of public procurement
- Open government portal, consists of: open data of government, open legal acts, open dialogue, open budgets, etc.
- All information on debt and guarantees made public

M&E = monitoring and evaluation; PPP = public–private partnership.

Source: Authors.

(b) Poor record-keeping has always been cited as a key problem area in the country's diagnostic work in the preparation of the CPSs, despite the presence of a FMIS at the center of government. By extension, then, publication of relevant information is also constrained, which fundamentally undermines the entire work on oversight and accountability. Causes of poor record-keeping also are reflected in old and dated information systems, or on differing platforms and the inability of these to communicate with each other. Thus, lapses in the quality of information are often cited in the GMaP assessment and diagnostic work at the country level.

Related to poor record-keeping, and drawing from it, are lapses in information not being disclosed. For example, reviews of the debt management situation invariably shed light on the lack of critical information on contingent liabilities of governments. This is a major lapse for it not only constrains good oversight but also puts at risk the entire fiscal stability framework in the PFM system.[119] There have been recent developments in analytical methods that enable data robustness using cost accounting data to strengthen PFM.[120] It is argued that application of this method in the PFM system will ultimately bolster budget credibility, performance-based budgeting, public procurement, and corruption detection (given the centrality of accounting for costs in these domains).

[119] In this regard, note the good practice in Georgia of not only robust databases but also the smooth flow of inter-government sharing of information. Following the Law of Georgia on Public Debt (Article 7), the MOF provides information to the National Bank of Georgia (NBG) on public debt and the loans for which State guarantees are issued. On a monthly basis, MOF provides information on public debt statistics (balance, disbursements, grants, etc.) to Parliament, the Government, and the NBG. The public debt statistics are also available on the MOF's website. On a monthly basis, the Treasury Service receives the current statistical data of the public debt and forecasts of future payments of the public debt from the department responsible for debt management.

[120] L. del Paso et al. 2025. Making Cost Accounting Data Work for Public Financial Management. *IMF Working Paper* WP/25/159. Washington, DC.

Often, the data and information generated does not fully and accurately capture the essence of the public policy being pursued. To counter this, the Lao PDR, for example, uses data for the Lao Social Indicator Survey to help inform better-designed and more-targeted inclusive education and gender equality policies.[121]

Countries also have noble provisions on access to information, but such access is limited either due to costs, or non-response from government agencies. For example, in Armenia, Nepal, and elsewhere, the right to access information is guaranteed by the Constitution, and there are even laws on such access, but it is difficult for the common person, or even active institutions (such as civic society) to get the needed information. Government agencies have been known to provide unreasonable or incomplete responses thus stymying the exercise of the right to information.

Finally, it is not always clear that governments are making use of data-driven measures to structure policies on service delivery enhancements. Hence, it can be said that if accountability is one of the core elements of good governance, and if accountability is ascertained only when the right information on (non-)lapses in government work is brought to light, then it follows that information systems (with the right data and information at their center) are the primary bases of what contribute to good governance.[122]

Lack of a Systems Perspective in Governance

The second backdrop to any discussion on the reform space on governance in general—and PFM and PSM, in particular—is the absence of a systems perspective in policymaking and implementation. This is not an infrequent occurrence; most DMCs reflect this in various ways. Indeed, the midterm review of ADB's Strategy 2030 brought out this point in a very clear and concise manner: "Multidimensional vulnerability...has become a critical element to consider when designing and delivering solutions for clients."[123] While that particular focus was on vulnerability, it can be argued that this is universally applicable in the public policy domains in DMCs.

At a more practical level, this can be seen as applicable in four specific ways, all of which have deep implications for how governance is to be enhanced across the board.

Not taking a whole-of-government perspective. Instances of where this is missing are evident in, for example, taking a unidimensional perspective on how to address malgovernance in the form of corruption in society.[124] All too often, relevant central agencies are focused on looking at corruption dimensions from a reactive pose (i.e., a case is filed or the anticorruption agency's attention is directed by the PAC to some matter highlighted in the auditor's report, and an investigation is commenced). Being proactive about how to stem such instances through measures that enhance ethics and integrity (or even as follow-ups to oversight results) would imply that a comprehensive approach is being taken. This point is detailed further below while discussing the concept of a national integrity system.

121 See, for example, Development Asia. 2025. Using Data to Build Inclusive Policies in Lao PDR (accessed 13 August 2025).

122 Measuring what matters is a fundamental challenge in public policy not just in DMCs, however. As a former Finance Minister of New Zealand once said while preparing the world's first "well-being budget": *"The things New Zealanders valued were not being sufficiently valued by the Government, and because they were not being valued, they were not being measured, and because they were not being measured, they were not being done."* (https://www.beehive.govt.nz/speech/minister-finance-wellbeing-budget-speech; accessed 22 July 2025).

123 Asian Development Bank. 2024a. *Strategy 2030 Midterm Review: An Evolution Approach for the Asian Development Bank*. p. 22.

124 Another is the absence of a strategic and holistic approach to looking at what is termed "intersectional marginalization," that is the various connections across different dimensions to understand why, for example, one group is further marginalized. A woman in an urban area, a woman in a rural area, and a Dalit (i.e., untouchable) woman with disabilities in a rural area face different realities of being marginalized, with the last individual suffering several layers of being so.

Not being able to "connect the dots." Even a cursory examination of the nine themes covered in this study show an immense range of interconnections that go to the heart of how and why a systems perspective is needed. In **Appendix 4**, these interactions are exemplified, a sample of which is provided in **Table 16**.

Table 16. Exemplification of Interconnections Across Thematic Areas

	Interconnections between...		Exemplified by
1	(1) Subnational governance	(7) Climate and Disaster Resilience	Local level CDR capacity is considerably lower than at the center
2	(4) Managing fiscal risks	(5) Private Sector Development	Fiscal risks from poorly designed PPPs
3	(8) Gender equality and social inclusion	(3) Public financial and public expenditure	MOF issues Gender Responsive Budgeting guidance for all agencies to follow
4	(6) Digitalization	(2) Domestic resource mobilization	Automation of tax systems helps in greater revenue mobilization
5	(9) Oversight & accountability	(3) Public financial and public expenditure	Robust systems (e.g., the TSA) and auditing provisions ensure better oversight of use of public funds

CDR = climate and disaster resilience, GESI = gender equality and social inclusion, MOF = Ministry of Finance, PPP = public–private partnership, TSA = treasury single account.
Source: Authors.

Missing out on furthering policy coherence in all development work. This is a very serious issue in all jurisdictions, but particularly so in DMCs. Related to the two points above, it refers to greater "capacity to design, implement, and monitor coherent and integrated policies."[125]

ADB's work in the 12 DMCs[126] of the Pacific region is an excellent example of a strong focus on policy coherence, and on taking an integrated whole-of-region approach. ADB's Pacific Approach takes into consideration the commonality of natural conditions in the 12 countries as well as their physical geographic size and location; these attributes include: "small population and land area, dispersion, isolation, and heightened exposure to disasters and the effects of climate change."[127] Their development challenges are also rather similar, including economic vulnerability, and capacity constraints. These are brought out in the issues/challenges they face in the domains of (a) domestic resource mobilization and debt management, (b) public finance and expenditure management, and (c) oversight and accountability (**Appendix 5**).

Not transcending beyond the one-to-one working group relationship among the donor community in DMCs. Donor partner coordination issues have always featured in all DMCs. Each partner has its own mandates, interests, and operating parameters; while coordination efforts exist, they do not normally tend to go beyond the specific working groups that individual parts of the agencies work on. **Box 20**, for example, documents three of the many working groups that have been formed by the donor community in Nepal. Yet while the group members are

[125] OECD's treatment on policy coherence is considered the gold standard in looking at how governments can further an integrated and comprehensive view of public policy (see https://www.oecd.org/en/topics/policy-coherence-for-sustainable-development.html; accessed: 21 August 2025).

[126] These DMCs include the Cook Islands, the Federated States of Micronesia, Kiribati, Nauru, Niue, Palau, the Republic of the Marshall Islands, Samoa, Solomon Islands, Tonga, Tuvalu, and Vanuatu.

[127] ADB. 2021b. *Pacific Approach 2021–2025*.

Box 20. Examples of Working Groups Among Development Partners in Nepal

Public Financial Management (PFM) Working Group

Its objective is to establish an adequate structure for enhancing coordination and collaboration in PFM initiatives and policy dialogue and generate knowledge collectively on PFM reform for decision-making. PFM is a sector that has a broader cross-cutting implication. The Working Group will build an interface with the government on PFM reform initiatives on fiscal federalism, produce knowledge and share it with the heads of missions and senior leadership to help them to understand the matter, effectively collaborate, and make informed decisions.

Accountability and Integrity Working Group

The Group has membership of development partners that are involved in supporting the government's anticorruption efforts and governance reforms in relevant areas. The Group specifically tries to advance implementation and institutionalization of the United Nations Convention Against Corruption through periodic review and implementation of their recommendations.

Public Asset Management Working Group

The Group enhances coordination to: (a) harmonize and promote joint approaches and standards in the areas of assets management within the development partners and government; (b) advance conceptual clarity of the asset management within them; (c) lead policy dialogue with the federal, provincial, and local governments to institutionalize asset management systems and practices; (d) synthesize and share this knowledge within and between the development partners and government; (e) develop asset management champions among them; and (f) serve as an expert group in asset management.

Source: Country diagnostic work for the Nepal CPS, 2024.

active amongst themselves this is more with respect to the mandates of that particular group, and not in relation to the interactions with the others.[128] This degree of segregation is the reason why governments get away with playing off donors against each other to secure projects that any one member of the donor group may have turned down.

What all these imply is that even as lapses exist in taking a systems perspective in governance, across the DMCs there are coordinating bodies at the center of government whose mandates are to enable such a perspective. In Bangladesh, for example, the Cabinet Division ensures that central level agencies in government are not only coordinating with each other but are doing so beyond in an administrative capacity. This is where the concept of information asymmetry helps explain how the imbalance in access to information, and acting on it, needs to be prioritized for a systems perspective to governance to be engendered in the public management domain.

It further implies that governments at all levels (i.e., center, provincial, and local) could also effectively guide the work of public sector entities to ensure that there is a well thought-through and robust M&E mechanism, as well as a mechanism to identify gaps, measure impact, enhance coordination, and guide policy adjustments. Transaction costs of doing so will be elevated in the initial stages but the downstream gains are substantial.

[128] For example, the PFM Working Group is not necessarily coordinated with the focus areas, and issues, in the Accountability and Integrity Working Group. Yet, clearly there are strong links between the two (e.g., weaknesses in the PFM system – flagged by the Office of the Auditor General – are not necessarily the domain of focus of the Working Group on Integrity; or even if it is, it is in passing since the same individual may be a member of both Working Groups).

Vectors and Frames of Actions

Considering the discussion above, the study identifies three vectors of opportunities (i.e., reform spaces, or pathways) that could be considered to strengthen PSMG across the DMCs. The subsequent discussion then looks at the specific frames of such action (i.e., a focus on the "how"). The pathways are applicable across levels of government (i.e., they apply as much at subnational level).

Vector 1: the first set of opportunities is inherent in the need to focus more substantively on strengthened country systems, greater macrofiscal stability, and greater PSD. Enhancement of these areas imply clearly the attainment of the strategic outcome of improved PSMG.

Vector 2: the second set of opportunities is contained in the strategic priorities determined earlier and draws inherently from Vector 1. As such, governance enhancement is evident in:

(a) *Accountability* through attention to oversight mechanisms (such as the work of the independent auditors at the Office of the Auditor General).
(b) *Inclusiveness*, primarily in GESI but also with strong government consideration of its pledge to leave no one behind.
(c) *Fiscal discipline, and fiscal transparency*, since the former implies evidence that governments are exercising care to ensure macroeconomic stability (e.g., by limiting excessive debt accumulation, or reducing exposure to volatile markets); and the latter ensures that governments are open about their fiscal situation, thus enabling a strong focus on the value of accountability of government.
(d) *Credible commitment* to PSD, including through robust PPPs, and creation of enabling conditions (such as on competition) in the market to facilitate private sector entry and growth.

Vector 3: the third set of opportunities focuses on the instruments that governments can optimize the use of so as to be able to meet higher level objectives, for example: (a) instituting a *National Integrity System* (NIS);[129] (b) *digitalization*, not just with respect to application of relevant technologies or developing comprehensive databases and information systems (important as they are) but with respect to service delivery since the primary function of governments is to serve all population groups; and (c) *strengthening civil society involvement* in the governance process.

It has been argued that accountability (particularly of governments to public resources used and results achieved) is critical for good governance. Since governments cannot be expected to be impartial in terms of setting decision metrics on their own degree of accountability, it is critical for civil society to play a more active role in ensuring this, a function they are primarily geared for. Helping them achieve their mandates (particularly when the civic operating space is deemed constrained) is what will be a prime instrument that can be used to institute good governance. Also, this study argues that it is far more impactful to put in place *ex-ante* provisions for monitoring policy implementation than to have CSOs involved in *ex-post* reviews of the same.

Action Frames

So, what actions can governments take from a more holistic angle that give effect to the sets of variables identified in the three vectors? Based on the findings of this study, four specific frames of action become evident to ADB and to the DMC governments when it comes to maximizing the opportunities to carry out the reforms that are needed.

[129] It is important to clarify that, even as NIS implies a macro perspective (and at the outcome level), this report puts forth the argument that – similar to the use of country systems being deemed an instrument of good governance than an outcome of good governance already achieved – so too does pursuing NIS from an instrumentation perspective imply that governments will engage in work that builds the foundational aspects of good governance which impact the pathways (i.e., Vector 2), and then eventually the outcomes (i.e., Vector 1).

These action frames (see **Figure 12**) in terms of intensity and scale of involvement and engagement can be seen as being hierarchically structured, thus:

(a) *Frame 1:* at the most direct level, strategic capacity building for, and support of, relevant entities that are directly associated with all relevant operations.
(b) *Frame 2*: at the second level, greater engagement with all entities that impinge on ADB's and the DMCs' operations, to ensure that everyone has a finger on the pulse of what is transpiring in the country and how lapses can best be addressed.
(c) *Frame 3*: in line with ADB's own Strategy 2030 (and its mid-term review) provisions, including those from individual DMC's vision for long-term goals, are areas where advocacy needs to be enhanced across the DMCs.
(d) *Frame 4*: to better understand the regional context, ADB as well as its DMCs will need to ensure emphasis on gaining better understanding of various on-the-ground realities of the way PSMG is practiced.

Figure 12. Action Frames for Consideration of ADB and Developing Member Country Governments

Frame 1
Strategic capacity building for & support of...

1. Strategic planning, PFM systems, oversight agencies
2. Strengthening information systems so that reporting and monitoring processes may be more robust
3. PFM related entities at the subnational level in DMCs where this has been found to be deficient
4. Domestic resource mobilization measures
5. Better management of procurement systems, particularly on sustainable public procurement

Frame 2
Greater engagement with...

1. Governments at all levels in order to be able to effectively address all concerns of mismanagement of resources as well as integrity-based systems
2. Non-government entities: (a) CSOs – at all levels; and (b) Private sector – various associations; as well as reform champions at all levels and across the country
3. Development partners: to enable targeted support for reforms in PSMG and in use of country systems

Frame 3
Enhanced advocacy of...

1. Integrated and holistic approach to national integrity systems (e.g., ethics in PSM)
2. Focus on enhancing transparency in the PFM and broader system; information asymmetry effectively smothers good governance
3. Strengthening skills as well as knowledge enhancement in legislative bodies intimately involved in PSMG areas
4. Greater push in DMCs for awareness on CDR and GESI

Frame 4
Better understanding of...

1. Issues that impact all facets of work on PSMG reforms (including use of country systems)
2. Role of non-traditional partners that can support reforms in PSMG areas on the ground
3. Context and contours of good practices elsewhere with the intent to replicate at home (e.g., impact of IT and digitalization efforts, funds flow management, etc.)
4. New ways of framing PSMG reform efforts in DMCs

ADB = Asian Development Bank; CDR = climate and disaster resilience; CSO = civil society organizations; DMCs = developing member countries; GESI = gender equality and social inclusion; IT = information technology; PFM = public financial management; PSMG = public sector management and governance.

Source: Authors.

Note the following sequencing of these action frames: strategic capacity building → greater engagement → enhanced advocacy → better understanding of. The first frame requires considerably more resources and knowledge/expertise to attain the objectives than the other three.

Learning from Others

There are a few implementation principles from regional and international experiences in the areas of macrofiscal and governance processes that all governments should give regard to. These stem not only from the positive experiences of the DMCs covered in this study, but also documented practices in other countries outside the study region including, for example, the UK, New Zealand, Estonia, Chile, etc. **Table 17** summarizes this information.

Table 17. Key Practices in Specific Countries on Aspects of Governance and Fiscal Policy

	Specific Area of Coverage	Country	Key Tools	Developing Member Countries in Asia and the Pacific
1	Fiscal rule enforcement	Chile	Autonomous Fiscal Council, legal compliance, public explanation of deviations	Anchor fiscal rules in law; establish advisory fiscal councils (even within MoF); require public explanation for deviations; build capacity for independent analysis over time.
2	Medium-term expenditure framework	South Africa	Rolling 3-year MTEF, annual updates, sectoral linkage	Pilot MTEFs in priority sectors; update annually; link to budget cycle; use regional peer learning (e.g., ASEAN+3, PIF) for capacity building.
3	Climate/disaster risk integration	Philippines	Climate budget tagging, fiscal risk statements	Start with simple climate budget tagging; include climate/disaster risks in fiscal risk statements; seek technical support from ADB/World Bank/UN; gradually expand coverage.
4	Digital/data integration	Estonia	X-Road interoperability platform, real-time data exchange	Develop national data exchange standards; prioritize integration of high-impact services (tax, procurement); participate in regional digital government initiatives (e.g., APEC, ASEAN).
5	GESI outcome measurement	Mexico	Gender budgeting with outcome indicators and public reporting	Define a small set of gender/inclusion outcome indicators; publish annual progress reports; involve local NGOs/women's groups in design and monitoring.
6	SOE/PPP fiscal risk management	New Zealand	Annual SOE stress tests, public risk registers, PPP contract transparency	Institutionalize annual SOE reviews; create public registers of PPP contracts/guarantees; engage with regional peers (e.g., Malaysia, Singapore) for knowledge exchange
7	Independent oversight	United Kingdom	Office for Budget Responsibility, formal public consultations	Start with semi-independent fiscal units in MOF; institutionalize public consultations (including digital platforms); leverage regional audit networks (e.g., PASAI) for support.

ADB = Asian Development Bank, APEC = Asia Pacific Economic Cooperation, ASEAN = Association of Southeast Asian Nations, DMCs = developing member countries, GESI = gender equality and social inclusion, MoF = Ministry of Finance, MTEF = medium-term expenditure framework, NGO = non-government organization, PASAI = Pacific Association of Supreme Audit Institutions, PIF = Pacific Island Forum, PPP = public–private partnerships, SOE = state-owned enterprise, UN = United Nations.

Source: ADB.

There are some principles, however, inherent in applying the lessons for other DMCs. These are rather self-evident in the study, and some key ones can be broadly summarized as follows.

- *Pilot first, scale up later.* Given that many reform efforts are new to a particular setting in the DMCs, it is necessary that a trial period precede the full-scale application of the efforts; the experiences of other countries have shown that DMCs may wish to first commence with a pilot before scaling up the reforms. Low absorptive capacity is a binding constraint in many DMCs, which implies the virtues of a pilot phase first.
- *Optimize regional organizations.* Use of regional organizations for peer learning and technical support could be enhanced. For example, the Pacific Islands Forum, which brings together 18 countries in the Pacific region, is a valuable resource for cross-country learning as well as technical support from countries such as Australia and New Zealand. The Forum brings together the Pacific countries to address pressing issues and challenges, including enabling robust public policy and a vibrant private sector. The Association of Southeast Asian Nations is another example of a strong regional organization that facilitates peer learning across its member countries and beyond the region.
- *Tailor reforms.* DMCs would do well to ensure that good practices evident elsewhere are not taken as copy-paste solutions. Examples abound of such practices that succeeded in one DMC setting not being so elsewhere.[130] All reforms to be copied from elsewhere must be tailored to suit the country context; indeed, these reforms are not necessarily best fit for all DMCs. As the noted economists Hausman, Rodrik, and Velasco opined back in 2006 "policies that work wonders in one place may have weak, unintended, or negative effects in other places."[131]
- *Prioritize transparency.* Good governance in all domains has one of its four underlying attributes as transparency (the others being accountability, participation, and rule of law). For governments to be held accountable for their policy actions (or inactions), and the results they produce (or do not, as the case may be), it is essential that the public has access to information. This is only possible when the degree of its transparency is high. Measures such as Freedom of Information (or Right to Information) Act, or digitalization, facilitate such access. This is if the system is robust and effective. Experiences of public policy action across the countries show that the degree of transparency—and the manner in which it is made available and communicated – is critical for good governance. Prioritizing transparency, thus, enables governments to demonstrate that they are credibly committed to policy reforms.
- *Leverage development partner support.* As DMCs begin to transition to middle-income (and even upper middle-income) countries, their capabilities to carry out comprehensive and complex reforms are also strengthened. Still, there is a significant role for bilateral and multilateral development partners to play in helping design and implement reform efforts, many of which require leveraging resources from outside the country. Development partners bring a lot to the table and not all of it just resources: their access to knowledge and technical capabilities means DMCs can maximize opportunities to ensure that their reform efforts bear fruit.

Concluding Remarks

Regardless of which frame of action ADB and its DMC governments see as the most relevant to governance operations on the ground, experiences in conceptualizing, strategizing, and implementing reforms across the DMCs (as reflected in ADB's internal analytical and country diagnostic work) have shown a few things:

130 See, for example, the warning from Allan Schick in his classic and well-regarded 1998 paper "Why most developing countries should not try New Zealand's Reforms." *The World Bank Research Observer.* 13, 1 (February): 123–31.

131 R. Hausman, D. Rodrik, and A. Velasco. 2006. Getting the Diagnostics Right. *Finance & Development.* 43(1): 12–15.

(a) Working collaboratively and strategically, with all development actors (including SNGs) yields better results, particularly in areas where reforms tend to be difficult.
(b) Greater focus on inclusiveness, broadly defined, will yield more desirable development outcomes; indeed, this is one of the intrinsic elements of ADB's Strategy 2030 and its mid-term review, as well as the development objectives of all DMCs.
(c) Consideration of intersectionality in reform efforts is critical, that is, how to enhance the welfare of marginalized women with disabilities, or how to incorporate climate or gender considerations in PFM systems is immensely more critical.
(d) An aggressive knowledge enhancement agenda, anchored on robust information systems, and greater impetus on facilitating data and information access lie at the heart of all governance reform efforts. Accountability of development results rests on the effectiveness of such an agenda.

In pushing for an agenda of strong good governance actions, taking into account the experiences of other DMCs has just as many advantages. This will mean, for example, that learning will more likely be a less expensive proposition than proceeding with experimentation without the tacit knowledge gained of others' experiences. In that sense, communities of practice, particularly across borders, are very valuable. A word of caution here, however – what works in one setting (even in technical areas such as macrofiscal domains) does not necessarily do so in another.[132]

The final observation has to do with political commitment. There are three factors essential to successful governance:[133] (a) strong and enduring political commitments to reforms; (b) technical capacity combined with initial insulation from political and societal pressures; and (c) incremental (gradual) rather than swift, broad reforms. But the overriding intangible is the commitment of political leaders to good governance, with particular focus on enhancing transparency and accountability. Indeed, such ***political commitment can be taken as a necessary and sufficient condition for good governance*** reforms in countries.

[132] Indeed, this is a key reason why this study shies away from the term "best practices" and insists on "good practices." The logic is to emphasize the notion of "good practice best fit" (see Ramalingam, et al. 2014, for a very concise treatment of this concept). In reviewing the analytical and country diagnostic work carried by ADB in recent years it is clear there is a bias, where it exists, towards best practices.

[133] M. Robinson. 2007. The Politics of Successful Governance Reforms: Lessons of Design and Implementation. *Commonwealth and Comparative Politics*. 45(4). pp. 521–548.

Appendix 1. Developing Member Countries Covered in the Study

This study is centered on the developing member countries (DMCs) of the Asian Development Bank (ADB). This report considers 34 DMCs for which ADB carried out diagnostic assessments (on, for example, governance risks and macrofiscal considerations) in the preparation of the country partnership strategies from 2021 to mid-2025. These DMCs can be categorized as in **Table A1.1**.

Table A1.1. Classification of the 34 Developing Member Countries Covered in the Study

		Classification According to Status of Access to Resources		
	Region	Group A (Concessional Assistance only)	Group B (OCR blend)	Group C (Regular OCR only)
1	Central and West Asia	Kyrgyz Republic	Uzbekistan	Armenia, Azerbaijan, Georgia, Kazakhstan, Turkmenistan
2	East Asia		Mongolia	
3	South Asia	Bhutan, Maldives, Nepal	Bangladesh, India, Sri Lanka	
4	Southeast Asia	Cambodia, Lao PDR	Timor-Leste	Indonesia, Philippines, Viet Nam
5	Pacific	Federated States of Micronesia, Kiribati, Nauru, Republic of the Marshall Islands, Samoa, Solomon Islands, Tonga, Tuvalu, and Vanuatu	Cook Islands, Fiji, Niue, Palau, Papua New Guinea	

DMC = developing member countries, OCR = Ordinary Capital Resources, Lao PDR = Lao People's Democratic Republic.

The following notes are relevant:

- Of the countries covered in this study, these are classified as Least Developed Countries (LDC) by the United Nations (as of December 2024): Bangladesh, Cambodia, Kiribati, the Lao PDR, Nepal, Solomon Islands, Timor-Leste, and Tuvalu. Of these, Bangladesh, the Lao PDR, and Nepal are scheduled to graduate out of LDC status in November 2026, Solomon Islands in December 2027, and Cambodia in December 2029. Source: https://www.un.org/development/desa/dpad/wp-content/uploads/sites/45/publication/ldc_list.pdf (accessed 10 August 2025).
- ADB classifies 11 DMCs as fragile and conflict-affected situations: Afghanistan, the Lao PDR, Myanmar, the Federated States of Micronesia, Kiribati, the Republic of the Marshall Islands, Nauru, Papua New Guinea, Solomon Islands, Timor-Leste, Tuvalu. With the exception of Afghanistan and Myanmar, all these DMCs are covered in this study.
- 16 DMCs identify as small island developing states: the Federated States of Micronesia, Kiribati, the Republic of the Marshall Islands, Nauru, Papua New Guinea, Solomon Islands, Timor-Leste, and Tuvalu. Cook Islands, Fiji, Maldives, Niue, Palau, Samoa, Tonga, and Vanuatu. (Source: ADB, 2021a). All the small island developing states are covered in this study.

Note: ADB placed its regular assistance to Afghanistan on hold effective 15 August 2021. Effective 1 February 2021, ADB placed a temporary hold on sovereign project disbursements and new contracts in Myanmar.

Source: ADB, Operations Manual, OM Section A1; as of July 2025.

Appendix 2. Schematic Flow: Use of Country Systems for Development Effectiveness

Figure A2.1. Analytical Frame for Situating the Use of Country Systems

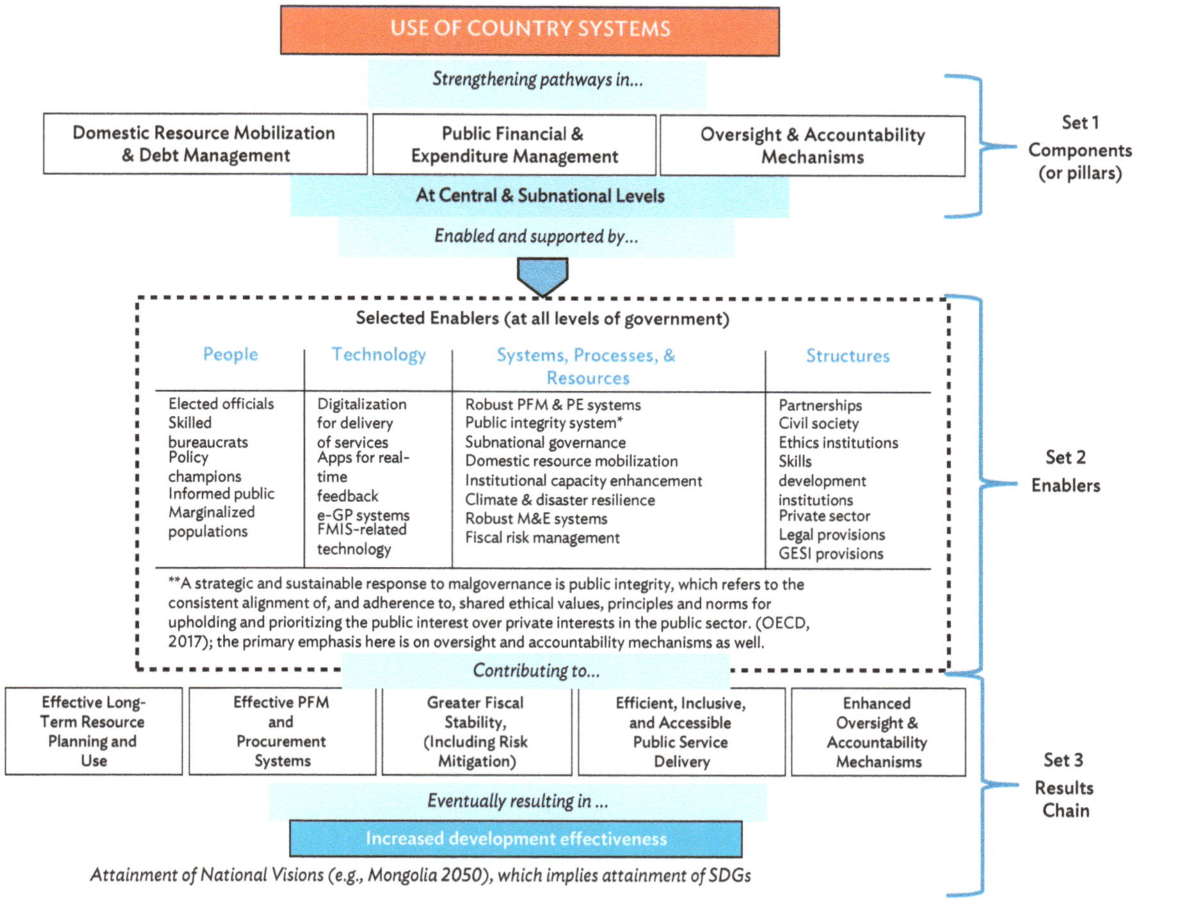

CSO = civil society organization, e-GP = electronic government procurement, FMIS = financial management system, GESI = gender equality and social inclusion, GPS = global positioning system, M&E = monitoring and evaluation, PE = public expenditure, PFM = public financial management, SDGs = Sustainable Development Goals.

Source: ADB's Country Diagnostic Work for the Nepal CPS (2025–2029), June 2024.

Notes on the representation on country systems:

(a) At a more operational level, the term refers to country systems that typically include, but are not restricted to, national arrangements and procedures for PFM (budgeting, treasury, accounting, auditing, and reporting), and for procurement (see OECD. 2011. *Using Country Public Financial Management System: A Practitioner's Guide.* Paris, p. 13).

(b) The three key sets of the representation focus on, respectively: components, enablers, and results chain.

(c) Note the focus on 'all levels of government,' *that is,* at central and subnational levels.

Appendix 3. Use of Country Systems—Decision Metrics

Table A3.1. Summary of Decision Metrics on Country Systems Elements and Degree of Usage

Domains	Element	Degree of Usage: Fully Used	Degree of Usage: Partially Used	Degree of Usage: Not Used
Public Financial Management	Budgeting	ADB financing, regardless of modality, is programmed through the country's system and is included in the national budget (and SNG, as applicable). Alternatively, programming is driven by country institutions, even if additional ADB- oriented documentation is required / produced.	ADB financing is included in the budget of the national government, but not in the budgets of the SNGs, where applicable	ADB financing is not included in the budgets of the government at any time or at any level
	Treasury	ADB funds are disbursed using the same treasury systems and banking arrangements used for disbursing the government's domestic resources. Alternatively, special accounts are used to manage ADB funds separately from the government's own resources, but disbursement processes are managed by country institutions through common treasury systems.	ADB funds are transferred to a special account under the government's consolidated fund and managed as agreed between ADB and the government.	ADB funds are transferred to an advance account at a bank and managed as per ADB's Loan Disbursement Handbook
Accounting		The government's accounting systems are used to manage, classify, and record ADB- financed program and project transactions, and produce financial reports that are accepted without any additional safeguards or reporting. Alternatively, ADB implements projects using the government's accounting systems, but requires government systems to be modified to allow tracking of program expenditure or additional reporting.	Project accounting follows the government's laws and regulations, and uses the existing accounts codes, but reporting is done using ADB's report formats	The accounting and reporting approach for ADB-financed projects does not apply the government's account codes, procedures, or reporting templates

continued on next page

Table A3.1 *continued*

Domains	Element	Degree of Usage		
		Fully Used	Partially Used	Not Used
	Auditing	ADB-financed programs and projects are audited by the government's auditing institution in accordance with country legal frameworks and audit frameworks and procedures. Alternatively, ADB uses the country's SAI but requires specific audits of donor programs, normally using ADB-specified terms of reference. Such additional audits may be carried out by the SAI's own staff or by a private firm approved and quality-assured by the SAI.	Project financial statements are audited by an independent audit firm engaged by, or on behalf of, the SAI but based on terms of reference approved by ADB	ADB-financed programs and projects are audited by private auditors hired by ADB or the contractor implementing the projects
	Reporting	ADB uses the government's reporting system and relies on the country's financial and nonfinancial reports and/or reporting standards and formats for its own monitoring and evaluation purposes. Alternatively, ADB's fund flows are reflected on government reports, even if ADB requires parallel reporting for its own fiduciary risks and strategic management purposes.	ADB uses the government's reporting system but requires additional reports from the government	ADB uses its own reporting systems and standards and ADB's fund flows are not reflected on government reports
Public Procurement	Procurement	All Open Competitive Biddings (OCBs) are done using the government's procurement rules, without imposition of additional or special requirements.	Some OCBs are conducted using the national system, for example, nationally advertised OCBs	All procurements follow ADB's procurement regulations

ADB = Asian Development Bank; OCB = open competitive bidding; SAI = supreme audit institution.

Source: Syquia, J. 2023. What Can Be Done to Improve the Use of Country Governance Systems? *The Governance Brief*. Issue 51. ADB: Manila.

Appendix 4. Stylized Cross-Interactions in Macrofiscal and Governance Domains

Table A4.1. Stylized Cross-Interactions in Macrofiscal and Governance Domains

	1. SNG	2. DRM	3. PFM & PE	4. Managing Fiscal Risks	5. PSD	6. Digitalization & Service Delivery	7. CDR	8. GESI	9. Oversight & Accountability
1. Subnational Governance									
2. DRM	Low OSR levels in SNGs								
3. PFM & Public Expenditures	SNGs not integrated into Treasury system	Robust PFM systems result in strong DRM efforts							
4. Managing Fiscal Risks	Fiscal risks from SNGs due to poor record-keeping	Fiscal risks elevated as DRM levels > *ex-ante* specifications	Fiscal risks arise from weak PFM and PE systems						
5. Private Sector Development (PSD)	General lack of systems and capabilities to energize PSD	Effective PSD will, in the long run, positively impact DRM	Robust PFM systems enable PSD thru SOE reforms	Fiscal risks from poorly designed PPPs					
6. Digitalization & Service Delivery	Accurate databases in SNGs facilitate service delivery	Automation of tax systems help greater revenue mobilization	Lapses in FMIS compromise effective PFM	Robust databases help better fiscal risk management	Digitalization helps minimize costs to governments of facilitating PSD				
7. CDR	Local level CDR capacity is lower than at the center	Robust DRM measures mean resources CDR	Integration of CDR into the PIM framework	CDR implies readiness for fiscal risks	Greater scope for private sector in post-disaster reconstruction	Robust information systems facilitate service delivery post-disasters			
8. GESI	GESI provisions in laws guide SNG actions	Stronger DRM means more resources for GRB	MOF issues GRB guidance for all agencies to follow	Lower fiscal risks, due to inclusion	Greater private sector role in developing women-owned small businesses	Greater access to digital technology for women in rural areas facilitates GESI measures	Gender impacts of CDR upfront		
9. Oversight & Accountability	Proximity to service recipients means greater accountability	Better oversight of DRM ensures more trust in PFM system	Robust systems (e.g., the TSA) ensure better oversight of public funds	Weak oversight leads to less effective management of fiscal risks	Effective oversight of market competition is essential for robust PSD	Proper use of digital technology greatly facilitates effective oversight mechanisms	Weak accountability of fund usage post- disasters	Weak oversight = weak GESI service delivery	

CDR = climate and disaster resilience, DRM = domestic resource mobilization, EPA = Environmental Protection Act, FMIS = financial management information system, GESI = gender equality & social inclusion, GRB = gender-responsive budgeting, MOF = Ministry of Finance, OSR = own source revenue, PE = public expenditure, PFM = public financial management, PIM = public investment management, PPPs = public–private partnerships, PSD = private sector development, SNG = subnational government, TSA = Treasury Single Account.

Source: Authors.

Appendix 5. Collated Notes on Macrofiscal and Governance Reforms in the Pacific Region

1. Domestic Resource Mobilization and Debt Management

Table A5.1. Notes on Macrofiscal and Governance Reforms in the Pacific Region

Notes from the GMaP assessment of the Pacific region, carried out in 2025, highlight several issues and challenges, as well as opportunities for reforms, in three domains of public sector and management: (1) domestic resource mobilization and debt management, (2) public financial and expenditure management, and (3) oversight and accountability. These are detailed below in Table A5.1.

Sub-Regional DMCs	Issues and Challenges	Opportunities for Systemic Improvements and Reforms
PLCO DMCs Nauru Solomon Islands Vanuatu	• Risks persist in revenue administration and forecasting, which, despite coordination between revenue authorities and finance ministries, still remain largely trend-based. Models also tend to not incorporate macroeconomic indicators or compliance behavior thus minimizing analytical depth of the forecasts. • Little estimation of tax gaps or systematic leakage assessments. • Data limitations, manual reconciliation processes, and outdated ICT systems hinder effectiveness of revenue operations. • Audit readiness and arrears tracking remain weak due to capacity constraints. • Across the region, implementation of transparency standards is uneven, with limited public reporting on beneficial ownership, accounting records, or progress on international obligations	• Accelerate digitalization of tax administration systems, with a focus on core functions, for example, registration, return filing, compliance monitoring • Develop tax gap estimation methodologies and integrate them into policy analysis and forecasting • Enhance variance analysis through formalized reporting processes. • Further integrate medium-term debt management strategies into fiscal frameworks, which includes improving the disclosure of contingent liabilities. • Participation in international tax transparency frameworks should be deepened through formal accession, compliance follow-up, and regional coordination

continued on next page

Sub-Regional DMCs	Issues and Challenges	Opportunities for Systemic Improvements and Reforms
SPSO DMCs Cook Islands Kiribati Niue Samoa Tonga Tuvalu	• Most DMCs do not estimate tax gaps or systematically quantify compliance risks such as tax evasion or fraud. • In a few DMCs audit and compliance functions remain underdeveloped due to limited capacity and outdated legislation. • Forecasting models in many DMCs do not fully incorporate compliance behavior or impact of tax incentives, resulting in reduced forecast precision. • Digital systems are also fragmented in some DMCs and taxpayer data is stored across multiple platforms, undermining data quality and the reliability of reporting. • Structured audit procedures are also found wanting in some DMCs, and staff shortages are also evident • Regarding international tax cooperation, a few DMCs have not joined either the Global Forum or the BEPS Inclusive Framework, which limits alignment with global standards. • Even among participating countries, implementation gaps remain, including incomplete availability of ownership, banking, and accounting records.	• Carry out institutionalizing tax gap analysis, enhancing digital tax administration systems, and integrating compliance risk into revenue forecasting. • Structured compliance strategies should be expanded to all DMCs, along with the implementation of internal audit units and performance tracking. • DMCs lacking formal frameworks should develop and publish debt strategies while enhancing public disclosure. • Those with existing strategies should strengthen operational monitoring, incorporate contingent liability tracking into fiscal frameworks, and improve inter-agency coordination to manage increasing risks related to climate and disaster financing.
North Pacific DMCs Federated States of Micronesia Palau Republic of the Marshall Islands	• Revenue forecasting methods still do not use macroeconomic modeling or sensitivity analysis. • No estimation of tax gaps or conduct of risk-based audits. • Internal audit functions within tax agencies are either underdeveloped or absent, and public reporting of audit results is inconsistent. • Compliance enforcement remains reactive rather than strategic. • International tax cooperation is limited. • Strategic planning is still uniformly underdeveloped. • Contingent liabilities are not adequately quantified or disclosed • Fiscal risk reporting remains fragmented. • Debt systems are not integrated with FMIS platforms, which limits analytical capabilities and responsiveness	• DMCs to adopt a regionally coordinated approach to modernize and digitalize tax administration—particularly by expanding automation beyond customs functions. • Establish formal revenue forecasting frameworks using econometric models • Enhance audit planning with risk-based approaches • Publish variance reports to bolster fiscal credibility • Secure membership in the Global Forum and BEPS Inclusive Framework; and beneficial ownership standards aligned with global transparency norms. • Develop comprehensive medium-term debt management strategy documents that include scenario analysis and integrate fiscal risk reporting with their FMIS.

continued on next page

2. Public Finance and Expenditure Management

Sub-Regional DMCs	Issues and Challenges	Opportunities for Systemic Improvements and Reforms
PLCO DMCs 1. Nauru 2. Solomon Islands 3. Vanuatu	• Medium-term planning remains underdeveloped across the sub-region (e.g., in absence of binding expenditure ceilings, lack of a functional MTBF), etc. • Budget preparation processes suffer from tight timelines and delayed submissions to legislatures; limits scrutiny. • While internal audit functions exist, institutional coverage remains weak, with some DMCs not having an operational internal audit system. • Audit units are also poorly resourced and lack independence. • PIM is fragmented, and budget documents often omit full life-cycle costing. • Procurement laws are in place but implementation and enforcement is weak. • Procurement planning is also generally weak, as evident in, for example: (a) fragmented or nascent e-procurement systems; (b) limited public access to procurement data; (c) market competition is constrained by limited bidder participation; and (d) contract management systems are underdeveloped, undermining value for money.	• To strengthen performance on public financial and expenditure management, it is critical to institutionalize MTEFs and integrate capital budgeting with fiscal strategy. • Improving budget credibility by enforcing expenditure controls, and publishing timely execution data. • Internal audit units should be formalized and adequately resourced to ensure comprehensive government coverage. • In procurement: (a) regulatory frameworks should be expanded to include all entities and projects; (b) procurement planning should be mandated and integrated with budget processes; and (c) e-procurement platforms should be standardized. • Enhancing data transparency, market access, and contract monitoring is essential for greater efficiency and accountability in public investment and procurement practices.
SPSO DMCs 1. Cook Islands 2. Kiribati 3. Niue 4. Samoa 5. Tonga 6. Tuvalu	• TSA structures remain fragmented in several DMCs, with multiple bank accounts limiting liquidity visibility. • Some weaknesses in cash forecasting, and rolling cash forecasts are inconsistently applied across the region. • Arrears tracking underdeveloped generally; only a few have established systems for monitoring aged payables. • Internal control frameworks are codified in most DMCs, but internal audit coverage uneven. Several lack standardized audit frameworks and lack capacity • Limited follow-up on audit recommendations. • PIM systems: economic analyses are not consistently applied, and life-cycle costing is seldom integrated into budgets. Appraisal results are also not routinely published which limits transparency. • Implementation challenges persist in procurement. E-procurement is either partial or absent in most DMCs, and data on procurement performance remains limited. • Contract management systems generally weak.	• There is need to fully institutionalize medium-term budgeting in some DMCs while enhancing performance-based linkages in others • TSA reforms should be completed across all DMCs, incorporating integrated reconciliation mechanisms and formal suspense account management. • Internal audit systems need to be standardized throughout the region, supported by training and the adoption of quality assurance frameworks. • In investment management, appraisal methodologies should be formalized, and the publication of evaluation results must be institutionalized. • Procurement frameworks should be enhanced through the rollout of e-procurement platforms, mandatory publication of procurement data, and professional development for procurement officials.

continued on next page

Sub-Regional DMCs	Issues and Challenges	Opportunities for Systemic Improvements and Reforms
North Pacific DMCs 1. Federated States of Micronesia 2. Palau 3. Republic of the Marshall Islands	• MTFFs are weakly institutionalized – with forward estimates embedded in policy lacking, and with limited medium-term costing. • Fiscal strategies remain fragmented – generally lack performance frameworks or scenario analysis. • Execution credibility is low as budget outturns deviate significantly from plans. • Execution data are not publicly disclosed, and systemic lapses hinder TSA integration and FMIS-tax linkage. • Internal control environments are underdeveloped; commitment controls are not applied comprehensively, and internal audit units have limited authority, independence. • Procurement is significantly weak – absence of, for example, dedicated procurement legislation, or weak enforcement • Market competition is low in procurement, and frequent use of single-source awards, including for high-value contracts. • Procurement plans and data on contract awards are rarely published, thus adversely affecting transparency. • Contract management is inconsistently documented, and procurement oversight bodies lack enforcement capacity.	• To strengthen public financial and expenditure management: (a) institutionalize medium-term fiscal and expenditure planning, (b) enhance the realism and transparency of budget execution, and (c) reinforce commitment control along with internal audit mechanisms. • Performance-informed budgeting tools and fiscal forecasting capacity using scenario-based modelling should be enhanced. • Urgent reform is necessary in procurement, including in: (a) framing a dedicated procurement law; and (b) enhancing systemic capacity to finalize, implement, and strengthen the revised framework. • Common priorities include standardizing procurement planning, enhancing market competition, publishing contract award data, and introducing centralized e-Procurement systems.

3. Oversight and Accountability

Sub-Regional DMCs	Issues & Challenges	Opportunities for Systemic Improvements and Reforms
PLCO DMCs Nauru Solomon Islands Vanuatu	• SAIs across the sub-region face constraints in operational autonomy, staffing, and budgetary control. • While ISSAIs are formally adopted, their application in audit execution remains inconsistent. • Quality control systems in auditing are lacking, and performance auditing is not institutionalized. • Also an issue is that of delays in audit follow-up and limited audit coverage of high-risk sectors such as extractives and SOEs. • Consolidated financial statements for SOEs are not regularly prepared, and audit coverage is uneven. • Enforcement of anticorruption measures remains weak, in part due to institutional fragmentation. • Low enforcement capacity is also a serious issue	• To address weak oversight and accountability, there is need to strengthen SAIs' financial and operational independence through legal safeguards, autonomous budget processes, and better recruitment measures • Risk-based audit planning and quality assurance systems should be institutionalized. • All audit mandates should include performance audits supported by ISSAI-aligned manuals. • Consolidated reporting for SOEs and subnational entities is a priority to improve fiscal risk oversight. • Anticorruption efforts require robust strategies, well-resourced agencies, whistleblower protection and asset recovery frameworks. • Increased public access to oversight outputs and formal follow-up mechanisms are also needed to enhance accountability and restoring public trust.

continued on next page

Sub-Regional DMCs	Issues & Challenges	Opportunities for Systemic Improvements and Reforms
SPSO DMCs Cook Islands Kiribati Niue Samoa Tonga Tuvalu	• DMCs exhibit varying levels of capacity; gaps in financial reporting and external oversight persist, despite the presence of legal frameworks. • Quality and timeliness of financial reporting are uneven; multiyear backlogs in audit completion, and one DMC has not met statutory deadlines despite legal obligations. • Accrual-based IPSAS adoption remains limited, and reconciliation practices vary across countries. • Suspense account management and disclosure of long-term liabilities are inconsistent • In some DMCs, in-year monitoring is either absent or informal, and commitment data are generally excluded from interim reports across the region. • Operational autonomy and independence of SAIs across the region are constrained across many DMCs • SAIs in several DMCs lack control over budgets or staff • Audit coverage is inconsistent and delayed (one DMC has not completed a government audit since FY2013/14) • Performance audit frameworks are underdeveloped. • Several countries lack mechanisms for following up on audit recommendations, and there is limited disclosure of non-compliance with financial reporting obligations. • Implementation of anticorruption policies is weak • Generally, enforcement capacity, agency coordination, and public accountability mechanisms remain limited.	• Primary focus needs to be placed on safeguarding the independence of SAIs through legal and procedural reforms, ensuring direct budget submissions to legislatures and autonomy in staffing. • Audit quality should be enhanced through risk-based planning, standardized performance audit frameworks, and formal quality assurance systems. • Public access to audit reports should be mandated, and follow-up mechanisms should be institutionalized. • For anticorruption efforts, countries should adopt or update national strategies, establish independent enforcement bodies, and strengthen whistleblower protection laws. • Civic engagement, transparency initiatives, and coordinated oversight are also required to reinforce accountability and integrity in the region's fiscal systems.
North Pacific DMCs Federated States of Micronesia Palau Republic of the Marshall Islands	Some PFM weaknesses include: (a) persistent delays in submitting annual financial statements; (b) lack of comprehensive balance sheet disclosure; and (c) uneven in-year monitoring systems, for example, reports sometimes omit commitment data Oversight of SOEs and SNGs is constrained by inconsistent reporting. Audit selection process is not risk-based. SAIs struggle with low staffing and outsourcing of audits, which delays financial reviews. Anticorruption mechanisms appear fragmented; for example: (a) there is no national anticorruption strategy or lead coordinating institution; and (b) whistleblower protections and asset recovery legislation are absent.	Establishing full legal safeguards and enabling direct legislative reporting and budget autonomy so as to enhance the independence and capacity of SAIs Institutionalize risk-based audit planning, and systems to follow-up on audit recommendations to be strengthened / incentivized. Consolidated financial reporting for SOEs and subnational governments should be implemented to improve fiscal transparency. National anticorruption strategies should be developed, supported by functional coordinating bodies, whistleblower protections, and legal instruments for asset recovery.

MTBF = medium-term budgetary framework, MTEF = medium-term expenditure framework, DMCs = developing member countries, FMIS = financial management information system, FY = fiscal year, PIM = public investment management, IPSAS = International Public Sector Accounting Standards, ISSAI = International Standards of Supreme Audit Institutions, PFM = public financial management, PIM = public investment management, PLCO = Pacific Liaison Country Office, SAI = supreme audit institution, SNG = subnational government, SOEs = state-owned enterprises, SPSO = South Pacific Sub-Regional Office, TSA = treasury single account.

Note: Fiji and Papua New Guinea, which are also included in the Pacific grouping for ADB programming purposes, are not included in this sub-grouping since they are covered separately given that ADB prepares an individual Country Partnership Strategy for these two DMCs. For the 12 Pacific DMCs, a joint Pacific Approach Strategy is prepared here.

Source: ADB. Country diagnostic for the Pacific Approach, April 2025.

References

Ariuntungalag, B. 2022. *Country Report: Mongolia*. Asian Disaster Reduction Center. Japan.

Asian Development Bank. 2025a. *Staff Guidance for Governance and Macrofiscal Pillars (GMaP) Assessment: Assessing and Aligning Country Governance and Macrofiscal Development Opportunities with ADB Operations*. Manila.

Asian Development Bank. 2025b. *Asian Development Outlook: Trade Uncertainty Challenges – Resilience in Asia and the Pacific*. Manila.

Asian Development Bank. 2025c. *Harnessing Digital Transformation for Good.* Asian Development Policy Report. Manila.

Asian Development Bank. 2024a. *Strategy 2030 Midterm Review: An Evolution Approach for the Asian Development Bank*. Manila.

Asian Development Bank. 2024b. *Basic Statistics.* Manila.

Asian Development Bank. 2023a. *Pacific Economic Monitor. December. Manila.*

Asian Development Bank. 2023b. *Climate Finance Landscape of Asia and the Pacific*. Manila.

Asian Development Bank. 2022a. TA completion report for TA 9158. Manila.

Asian Development Bank. 2022b. *Sea-Level Change in the Pacific Islands Region: A Review of Evidence to Inform Asian Development Bank Guidance on Selecting Sea-Level Projections for Climate Risk and Adaptation Assessments*. Manila.

Asian Development Bank. 2021a. *Fragile and Conflict-Affected Situations and Small Island Developing States Approach: A Summary*. Manila.

Asian Development Bank. 2021b. *Pacific Approach, 2021–2025*. Manila.

Asian Development Bank. 2019a. *Public–Private Partnership Monitor*. 2nd edition. Manila. Washington, DC.

Asian Development Bank. 2019b. *Mongolia: Strengthening Capacity on Disaster Risk Assessment, Reduction, and Transfer Instruments in Mongolia.* Manila.

Asian Development Bank. 2018a. *Strategy 2030: Achieving a Prosperous, Inclusive, Resilient, and Sustainable Asia and the Pacific*. Manila.

Asian Development Bank. 2018b. *Asian Development Outlook 2018: How Technology Affects Jobs*. Manila.

Asian Development Bank. 2017a. *Asian Development Outlook 2017: Transcending the Middle-Income Challenge*. Manila.

Asian Development Bank. 2017b. *Fast-Track Tax Reform: Lessons from Maldives*. Manila.

Asian Development Bank. 2015. *Promoting the Use of Country Systems in ADB's Operations: A Systematic Approach*. Manila.

Asian Development Bank. 2011. *Asia 2050: Realizing the Asian Century*. Manila.

Bangladesh Bank. 2024. *Annual Report, 2023–2024*. Dhaka.

Bhatnagar, S. 2015. Using ICT to Improve Governance and Service Delivery to the Poor, (pp. 296–322) in B. Deolalikar, S. Jha, and P. Quising (eds), *Governance in Developing Asia: Public Service Delivery and Empowerment*. ADB, and Edgar Elgar Publishing, Cheltenham, UK.

Bhatta, G. 2021. Report on Country Context of Nepal. *UNDP Independent Country Evaluation for Nepal*. Independent Evaluation Office, UNDP, New York.

Bhatta, G. 2020. *Those that fix the lights...: The Practice of Public Sector Management in Developing Asia*. ADB, ADBI, Routledge. Manila, Tokyo, London.

Bhatta, G., and R. Huseynov. 2024. *Green Skills Development in Vocational Education & Training in Azerbaijan*. Policy Issue Paper for TA 6651 Azerbaijan: Strengthening Knowledge Management for More Effective Economic Policies. Baku, Azerbaijan.

Bicenio, B., and N. Bangsal. 2016. *Climate Budget Tagging: A Good Start Towards Tracking International Climate Finance Within the National Budget Process*. Philippines House of Representatives, CPBRD Discussion Paper, Issue no. 3.

Bova E., et al. 2016. The Fiscal Costs of Contingent Liabilities: A New Dataset. *IMF Working Paper*, WP/16/14. Washington, DC.

Center for Policy Dialogue. 2024. *White Paper 2024 – State of the Bangladesh Economy: Dissection of a Development Narrative*. Dhaka.

Center for Social Change. 2023. *Disaster Risk Governance*. Kathmandu.

Cobham, A., and P. Janský. 2017. Global Distribution of Revenue Loss from Tax Avoidance: Re-Estimation and Country Results. *WIDER Working Paper 2017/55*. Helsinki: World Institute for Development Economics Research.

del Paso, L, et al. 2025. *Making Cost Accounting Data Work for Public Financial Management*. IMF Working Paper WP/25/159. Washington, DC.

Deloitte Consulting. 2022. *Nepal Digital Services Sector: Market Systems Assessment.* USAID Trade and Competitiveness Activity. Kathmandu.

Deolalikar, A., and S. Jha, and P. Quising (eds). 2015. *Governance in Developing Asia: Public Service Delivery and Empowerment*. Manila: Asian Development Bank, and Cheltenham, UK: Edward Elgar.

Department of Foreign Affairs & Trade. 2024. *PNG Climate FIRST (Climate Finance Initiative for Resilience and a Sustainable Transition)*. Investment Design Document. Canberra.

Department of Foreign Affairs & Trade. 2019. *Assessing and Using Partner Government Systems for Public Financial Management and Procurement: Guideline*. Canberra: Government of Australia.

Fainboim, I., and I. Lienert. 2018. *The Macrofiscal Function and its Organizational Arrangements*. Technical Notes and Manuals. IMF: Washington, DC.

Fatas, A. et al. 2025. Dynamic Effects of Fiscal Rules: Do Initial Conditions Matter. *Policy Research Working Paper 11066*. World Bank, Washington DC.

Ferrarini, B., et al. 2022. *The Sustainability of Asia's Debt: Problems, Policies, and Practices*. ADB and Edward Elgar, Manila and Cheltenham, UK.

Giardino, A. 2025. Navigating the Rising Tide: Transformational Adaptation for Resilient Atoll Nations. *Development Asia Insight*. 25 March. Manila.

Goel, R., and J. Saunois. 2017. Forms of Government Decentralization and Institutional Quality: Evidence from a Large Sample of Nations. In N. Yoshino, and P. Morgan (eds), *Central and Local Government Relations in Asia: Achieving Fiscal Sustainability*, Cheltenham, UK, and Northampton, USA: Edward Elgar Publishing. pp. 395–419.

Government of Indonesia. 2023. *Digital Indonesia: Vision 2045*. Ministry of Communication and Informatics, Jakarta.

Government of Indonesia, and USAID. 2021. *Two Decades of Fiscal Decentralization Implementation in Indonesia*. Jakarta.

Government of Nepal. 2082 (2024/2025). Public Procurement Monitoring Office Annual Report. Kathmandu.

Government of Turkmenistan. 2023. *Voluntary National Review of Turkmenistan*. Ashgabat.

Hausmann, R., D. Rodrik, and A. Valasco. 2006. Getting the Diagnostics Right. *Finance and Development*. 43(1). pp. 12–15.

International Monetary Fund. 2025. *Fiscal Monitor.* April. Washington, DC.

International Monetary Fund. 2023. *Public Procurement in South Africa: Issues and Reform Options*. Washington, DC.

International Monetary Fund. 2021a. *Debt Guarantees and Loans Assessment Tool, Fiscal Risks Toolkit.* Washington, DC.

International Monetary Fund. 2021b. *Nepal – PIMA Climate Change Module, 2021.* Washington, DC.

International Monetary Fund. 2020. *Republic of Kazakhstan, Selected Issues.* Country Report No. 20/38. Washington DC.

International Monetary Fund. 2019. *Republic of Armenia: Fiscal Transparency Evaluation.* Washington, DC.

International Monetary Fund. 2018. *Vietnam, Public Investment Management Assessment – PIMA.* Washington DC.

International Monetary Fund. 2015. *Making Public Investment More Efficient.* Washington, DC.

Kar, D., and S. Freitas. 2012. *Illicit Financial Flows from Developing Countries: 2001-2010.* Washington, DC: Global Financial Integrity.

Low, J. 2016. Singapore's Whole-of-Government Approach in Crisis Management. *Ethos.* Civil Service College, Singapore.

Morgan, P., and L. Trinh. 2017. Frameworks for Central-Local Government Relations and Fiscal Sustainability, (pp. 3–63) in N. Yoshino, and P. Morgan (eds), *Central and Local Government Relations in Asia: Achieving Fiscal Sustainability.* Cheltenham, UK, and Northampton, US: Edward Elgar Publishing.

Nakatani, R. 2025. Preventing Fiscal Crises under Decentralization: Intergovernmental Policies and Institutions. *IMF Working Paper* 25/87, Washington, DC.

National Economic and Development Authority. 2023. *Philippine Development Plan 2023–2028.* Manila.

OECD. 2011. *Using Country Public Financial Management System: A Practitioner's Guide.* Paris.

OECD and ADB. 2023. *Multi-level Governance and Subnational Finance in Asia and the Pacific.* OECD Regional Development Papers. Paris, and Manila.

Pacific Region Infrastructure Facility. 2013. *Infrastructure Maintenance in the Pacific: Challenging the Build-Neglect-Rebuild Paradigm.* Sydney: Pacific Infrastructure Advisory Center.

Patel, S. et al. 2021. *Tackling Gender Inequality and Climate Change through the Budget: A Look at Gender-Responsive Climate Change Budgeting in Bangladesh and Mexico.* International Budget Partnership, Washington, DC.

Qian, Y., and G. Ronald. 1998. Federalism and the Soft Budget Constraint. *American Economic Review.* 88(5). pp. 1143–1162.

Republic of the Philippines. 2025. Philippines Disaster Resilient and Responsive-Public Financial Management (DRR-PFM) Assessment Report. Manila.

Ramalingam, B., et al. 2014. *From Best Practice to Best Fit: Understanding and Navigating Wicked Problems in International Development.* ODI Working Paper.

Robinson, M. 2007. The Politics of Successful Governance Reforms: Lessons of Design and Implementation. *Commonwealth and Comparative Politics*. 45(4). pp. 521–548.

Rozenberg, J. and M. Fay. 2019. *Beyond the Gap: How Countries can Afford the Infrastructure They Need While Protecting the Planet*. Sustainable Infrastructure. Washington, DC: World Bank.

Schick, A. 1998. "Why most developing countries should not try New Zealand's Reforms." *The World Bank Research Observer*. 13, 1 (February): 123–31.

Schwartz, G., et al (eds). 2020. *Well Spent: How Strong Infrastructure Governance Can End Waste in Public Investment*. IMF: Washington, DC.

Syquia, J. 2023. What Can Be Done to Improve the Use of Country Governance Systems? *The Governance Brief*. Issue 51. ADB: Manila.

Tanzi, V. 1997. The Changing Role of the State in the Economy: A Historical Perspective. *IMF Working Paper*, WP/97/114. Washington, DC.

Turkewitz, J., et al. 2018. *Improving Efficiency in Public Procurement in Georgia Findings from Data Analysis of Public Procurement Transactions in Georgia 2013-2016*. World Bank. Washington, DC.

UNCTAD. 2021. *Implementing Supportive Policies to Build a Vibrant Private Sector as a Driver of Structural Transformation*. Policy Brief, No. 89, October.

UNCTAD. 2020. *The Least Developed Countries Report 2020: Productive Capacities for the New Decade*. United Nations publication, Sales No. E.21.II.D.2, Geneva.

UNESCAP. 2019. *Readiness Assessment for Cross-border Paperless Trade: Mongolia*. Bangkok.

Weingast, B. 2009. Second Generation Fiscal Federalism: The Implications of Fiscal Incentives. *Journal of Urban Economics*. 65(3). pp. 279–293.

World Bank. 2022. Disaster Resilient and Responsive Public Financial Management: An Assessment Tool. Washington, DC.

World Bank. 2021. *PPP Legal, Regulatory and Institutional Framework Gap Analysis in Lao PDR*. Vientiane.

World Bank Group. 2014a. *The World Bank Group and Public Procurement: An Independent Evaluation*. Washington, DC.

World Bank. 2014b. *The World Bank and Public Procurement – An Independent Evaluation. Volume II: Achieving Development Effectiveness through Procurement in Bank Financial Assistance*. Washington, DC.

Yoshino, N., and P. Morgan (eds). 2017. *Central and Local Government Relations in Asia: Achieving Fiscal Sustainability*. Cheltenham, UK, and Northampton, US: Edward Elgar Publishing.

www.ingramcontent.com/pod-product-compliance
Lightning Source LLC
Chambersburg PA
CBHW041756220926
51847CB00014B/219
9789292777364